The Juridification of Religion?

Law and Religion

Volumes published in this Brill Research Perspectives title are listed at *brill.com/rplr*

The Juridification of Religion?

By

Helge Årsheim and Pamela Slotte

BRILL

LEIDEN | BOSTON

Originally published as Volume 1(2) 2017, in *Law and Religion*, DOI 10.1163/24682993-12340002.

Library of Congress Control Number: 2017955987

Typeface for the Latin, Greek, and Cyrillic scripts: "Brill". See and download: brill.com/brill-typeface.

ISBN 978-90-04-34962-9 (paperback)
ISBN 978-90-04-35986-4 (e-book)

This book is printed on acid-free paper and produced in a sustainable manner.

Contents

The Juridification of Religion?

Helge Årsheim
University of Oslo, Norway
helge.arsheim@teologi.uio.no

Pamela Slotte
Åbo Akademi University, Finland
pamela.slotte@abo.fi

Abstract

This article sets out to explore the extent to which developments currently taking place at the interface between law and religion in domestic, regional and international law can be conceptualized as instances of larger, multidimensional processes of juridification. We rely on an expansive notion of juridification, departing from the more narrow sense of juridificiation as the gradually increasing "colonization of the lifeworld" proposed by Jürgen Habermas in his *Theory of Communicative Action* (1987; Vol. 2, Beacon Press). More specifically, the article adapts the multidimensional notion of juridification outlined by Anders Molander and Lars Christian Blichner in their article 'Mapping Juridification' (2008; 14 *European Law Journal* 36), and develops it into a more context-specific notion of juridification that is attendant to the specific nature of religion as a subject matter for law.

Keywords

Juridification – law – religion – legal theory – constitutionalism – human rights

---

Helge Årsheim's research has been made possible by a grant from the SAMKUL programme of the Research Council of Norway. Slotte's research has been made possible by her Academy Research Fellow project "Management of the Sacred: A Critical Inquiry" (Academy of Finland, 2013–2018).

 | DOI 10.1163/9789004359864_002

Introduction

Religion is an "essentially contested concept", in the sense that it has "no one clearly definable general use".[1] Nevertheless, religion has increasingly become subject to legal regulation and adjudication, and the terms and procedures of law have become inevitable to political and social battles for the expansion or restriction of the role of religion in society. Indeed, public discourses on religion have largely come to depend on the vocabulary of legal regulations, legal modes of reasoning and legal decisions as shared starting points for deliberations on the nature, scope and role of religion in society. In this article, we explore the scope, origins and consequences of the increasing regulation and adjudication of religion, how the indeterminacy of both "law" and "religion" is handled within different legal areas, and how legal frames for religion travel across the legal system.

Guiding this investigation is the theory and concept of *juridification*, the process by which the scope of law gradually expands to new areas of social interaction, causing widespread social and political change in its wake. Despite the large and growing scholarly interest in the interrelationship between law and religion, scholars working in the field have yet to explore the potential of juridification as a tool of analysis.[2] This deficiency is not exclusive to law and religion scholarship, as juridification has still to gain any substantial traction as an established analytical concept. Lacking the hallmarks of a proper "buzzword", from the requirement that it should speak to a "primary audience" and provide a "novel twist to an old problem", to the bridging of a gap between generalists and specialists, juridification has remained a theory and concept of special, not general interest.[3] The only characteristic juridification appears to share with successful buzzwords like "post-secularism" or "intersectionality" is its inherent ambiguity and obviously incomplete, open-ended scope, as indicated by its fuzzy borders to neighbouring concepts like judicialization, politicization, legalization, constitutionalization and similar constructs.

Noting these challenges, Lars Christian Blichner and Anders Molander have suggested that a multidimensional approach may help sorting out the many

1 Walter B. Gallie, 'Essentially Contested Concepts' (1956) 56 *Proceedings of the Aristotelian Society* 167, 168.

2 Although Russell Sandberg, one of the leading theoreticians of the field, has made fleeting references to "juridification" in his writings as a process that is taking place in relation to religion, he has yet to apply the different aspects of the theory to the field.

3 Kathy Davis, 'Intersectionality as Buzzword: A Sociology of Science Perspective on What Makes a Feminist Theory Successful' (2008) 9 *Feminist Theory* 67, 70–77.

different layers of writings on juridification and related questions, developing a "conceptualisation that is complex enough to grasp the different meanings of the term and still simple enough to work as an inter-subjective standard",[4] offering a "prolegomena to a theory" of juridification that can account for the nature, origins and consequences of legal change. Disentangling the voluminous scholarly literature on the growth of legal regulation and adjudication, Blichner and Molander have developed a descriptive model of juridification that is spread across five different dimensions: (1) constitutional change, (2) expansion and differentiation of law, (3) increased conflict resolution by recourse to law, (4) increased judicial power, and (5) increased legal framing. Importantly, neither of these dimensions is monolithic or clear-cut, and their internal relationship is nonlinear and unpredictable, rendering the model a rough sketch at best.

Despite the simplifications inherent to the modelling of already complex and abstract concepts, we suggest that the model of juridification developed by Blichner and Molander can offer important new insights to scholars working at the multiple intersections of law and religion. A deeper engagement with the terms and conceptual divisions of this model can help identifying a range of new research questions, broadening the engagement between the field of law and religion and scholarship in other fields. More specifically, we suggest that an engagement with a multidimensional theory of juridification can assist scholars of law and religion in three distinct, yet interrelated areas.

First, approaching the interactions between law and religion with the multidimensional optics offered by Blichner and Molander invites new questions of how, when, where and why different regulations and adjudications of religion occur, and how they interact with one another. Viewing juridification as a mechanism in which a range of different, interlinked processes are set in motion whenever change occurs at either level of the model opens up a comprehensive, broad-based approach to the interaction between law and religion that considerably expands the conceptual horizon of scholarship on law and religion.

Second, importing the terminology and conceptual architecture of juridification, which has been developed as an attempt to account for legal change in general, serves to connect scholarship on law and religion with the broader fields of legal theory and socio-legal studies. A connection with the wider field of legal studies can serve to activate the tantalizing questions that lie at the

4 Lars Chr. Blichner and Anders Molander, 'Mapping Juridification' (2008) 14 *European Law Journal* 36, 37.

heart of any legal scholarship, such as "what is law, what is a legal order and how developments of law and legal orders may be understood".[5]

Third, and crucially, a multidimensional model of juridification invites the critical interrogation of some of the foundational themes in the scholarship on law and religion, the majority of which have been framed against the backdrop of earlier scholarship on ecclesiastical law, the relationship between church and state, and the conditions for individual and collective religious freedom and non-discrimination. These themes range from the discussion of whether we are currently witnessing the formation of "religion law" as a separate legal field, via the more or less taken for granted "special"' status of religion for regulatory purposes and the capacity of law to capture the modalities of "lived religion", and to the relevance of secularization and increased religious diversity to the changes in legal regulation and adjudication of religion (see below). These propositions have largely been formed on an underexamined premise of "the rule of law" as a stable foundation of legal order, ignoring decades of critical legal scholarship pointing to the inherently conflictual nature of modern legal regulation and adjudication. Opening up a conversation between theories of juridification and scholars of law and religion can help contextualize these themes, and examine their convergence or divergence with other developments in legal scholarship.

Much in the same way as the model of juridification which has served as the key inspiration for this article, our approach is inherently exploratory. Our primary purpose is to invite scholars of law and religion to consider the benefits of expanding their terminological and conceptual toolkit by appropriating and further discussing the applicability of juridification in general, and the model of juridification developed by Blichner and Molander specifically. We do not pretend to give an exhaustive account of the many different ways in which juridification may interact with scholarship on law and religion, but limit our inquiry to some of the principal issues that have arisen in our own work.

In the following sections, we discuss (1) the concept of juridification in general terms, before moving on to (2) an appreciation of some of the key debates in the growing scholarship of law and religion. In part (3), which is the main section of the article, we explore different ways in which the dimensions established in the model of juridification developed by Blichner and Molander may be applied in scholarship of law and religion, while also suggesting new questions and approaches that have so far not been thoroughly examined in the field. We also suggest different ways in which the dimensions interact, which is one of the key advances offered by a multidimensional account of law and religion.

5 Blichner and Molander 2008, 37.

1 Unpacking Juridification

Juridification is a slippery notion. The term in itself, while commonly associated with the work of Jürgen Habermas, can be traced back to (at least) the time of the Weimar republic, when it was used polemically to criticize the legal formalization of labour relations, leading to the neutralization of political class conflicts and the "petrification" of the political dynamics within the working class movement.[6] Although the term was new, the idea was old, continuing a longer interest in the ambivalent force represented by the increasing power of the legal system among earlier theoreticians of socialism: The pitfalls and prospects of an increased role for law had been explored by Friedrich Engels and Karl Kautsky in 1887, in the article "Juristen-Sozialismus" ["Juridical Socialism"]. In this article, Engels and Kautsky likened "the juridical world view" that developed in France in the 18th century to a "secularization of theology", as human justice replaced divine law and the state assumed the role of the church.[7] The observation that the religious worldview was about to be replaced by a no less menacing "juridical worldview" was not new to the socialist project, but had appeared already in Karl Marx' *On the Jewish Question* in 1843, where Marx sought to come to terms with the prospects of an emancipation of the Jews in Germany within the legal order of a Christian state. Despite the corruptive potential of law, however, Engels and Kautsky saw the need for "certain legalistic demands" emanating from active socialist parties, while also warning that these demands must be considered "variable elements" that need revisions from time to time.[8]

The view of a "juristic worldview" as a secularized version of an earlier religious worldview resonates with the work of legal historian Harold Berman, who localized the shift from the latter to the former even earlier, at the time of the "Papal Revolutions" in the 11th century, which ushered in a dualistic legal order for the first time in Western history.[9] In a different, more pragmatic vein, David Saunders has used juridification to describe the early modern development of a positive legal order detached from divine sanction in 17th century

6 Günther Teubner, 'Juridification—Concepts, Aspects, Limits, Solutions' in Günther Teubner (ed), *Juridification of Social Spheres: A Comparative Analysis in the Areas of Labor, Corporate, Antitrust and Social Welfare Law* (Walter de Gruyter 1987) 9.

7 Friedrich Engels and Karl Kautsky, 'Juridical Socialism' (1977 [1886]) 7 *Politics & Society* 203, 204.

8 Engels and Kautsky 1977 [1886], 219–20.

9 Harold J. Berman, *Law and Revolution: The Formation of the Western Legal Tradition* (Harvard University Press 1983) 118.

England and Germany, in what he considers to be an instrumental need to "protect the stability of civil life from known sectarian dangers".[10]

Depictions of the increasing role of law prior to the late modern period paint a picture of juridification as consisting primarily of (1) the differentiation of law as a separate regulatory system detached from its earlier connections with religion and (2) the hegemony of law as the primary regulatory system of modern nation states. Whereas (1) has largely receded into the background in contemporary accounts of the increasing power of law, (2) represents the most widely-held perception of what juridification entails. This is in no small part due to the theory developed by Jürgen Habermas in his *Theory of Communicative Action* (1987),[11] where he took the increasing hegemony of law as his starting point while developing his notion of juridification as one of the processes leading to the "colonization of the lifeworld" under conditions of late modernity.

Although juridification is only one small part of the large-scale theory of modernity and rationality Habermas laid out in the *TCA*, it plays a central role as the key process propelling the "technical" rationality of law to the centre stage of social organization, displacing the "instrumental" rationality of each social sphere falling under its regulation. According to Habermas, the ascendancy of law is particularly heartfelt in areas formerly outside the remit of formal legal organization, notably the family, upbringing and education. In these fields, ever larger portions of the lifeworld become subject to legal regulations implemented in order to secure the basic rights guaranteed by the modern welfare state.

However, due to the inherent differences between a technical, legal rationality bound by the rules and procedures of the legal system and the instrumental rationality that governs the day-to-day workings of the spheres under regulation, this "juridification" ends up in a dilemma: Securing the rights of individuals within the family structure provides them with the legal tools to stake their claims before the legal system—but the presence of these tools, which relate to each family member in isolation, threatens the cohesion of the family structure, whose very preservation is central to the purpose of legislative action in the first place.

As Daniel Loick has pointed out, this conception of juridification ignores the very real level of legal regulation within these fields in earlier times, and also pays scant attention to the political movements fostering the rights that

10 David Saunders, 'Juridifications and Religion in Early Modern Europe: The Challenge of a Contextual History of Law' (2004) 15 *Law and Critique* 99, 110.

11 Jürgen Habermas, *The Theory of Communicative Action*, vol. 2 (Beacon Press 1987).

have been implemented through law.[12] According to Loick, the problems represented by the encroachment of legal rules on ever larger parts of social life is better captured by the "paradox of rights" observed by Wendy Brown in relation to gender issues, where the recognition as liberal subjects requires a degree of abstraction and transcendence from the social construction of femaleness, as the ethos of the liberal state appears to be "socially masculine".[13]

In an alternative account of the challenges represented by the increasing role of law, Günther Teubner has characterized juridification as a necessary corollary of "societal evolution", under which different spheres of society undergo processes of increasing functional differentiation. In this evolutionary process, the "structural coupling" between politics and law, under which the political system regularly furnishes the legal system with new laws, is increasingly complemented by the specific challenges of the social spheres undergoing regulation, with the economic system as the primary example. Seeking to describe the complexity of a political system figuring out the regulatory challenges within a separate system using the tools and mechanisms of the legal system, Teubner has coined the phrase "regulatory trilemma".[14] Moving beyond the law/society nexus central to Habermas, Loick and Brown, Teubner highlights the interactions and translational difficulties that regularly occur at the intersections between multiple complex social systems, all of which are governed according to their own, internal logic. To ameliorate these challenges, Teubner suggests that law-making must abandon its hierarchic control of complex, self-reproducing systems in favour of a more indirect method of "decentral context regulation".[15] Such regulation would see the organization of social systems becoming subject to increasing "internal legal modelling", whereby each social system would internalize legal rules according to its own strategic variables,[16] in what would amount to a slightly refined version of the "variable elements" of law advised by Kautsky and Engels one hundred years earlier (see above).

Whereas the discussion of juridification at the structural level has largely dealt with law in somewhat abstract terms, another strain in the literature has emphasized the specific role of courts as key actors in the interaction between politics and law, pre-eminently captured by the term *judicialization*, with *juristocracy* or *courtocracy* among the negative epithets used to denote the possible

12 Daniel Loick, 'Juridification and Politics: From the Dilemma of Juridification to the Paradoxes of Rights' (2014) 40 *Philosophy & Social Criticism* 757.

13 Loick 2014, 772.

14 Teubner 1987, 21.

15 Teubner 1987, 39.

16 Teubner 1987, 39.

endpoints of the increasing power of courts and their judges.[17] The prime example of the political power of judges in this literature is the gradual increase since the Second World War in the number of states allowing judicial review, whereby courts can strike down laws passed by government if they are found to be in violation of some higher statute, most commonly the constitution.[18] Over the course of the last decades, the growing power of courts through increased judicial review has been further expanded by the influence of transnational courts and tribunals, pre-eminently the European Court of Human Rights (ECtHR) and the European Court of Justice (CJEU), the decisions of which can be used to challenge existing and pending legislation in a growing number of European states.

The growth in judicial review and the influence of transnational tribunals have lifted power from the legislative branch and granted it to the judiciary, whose increasing dominance has also been characterized as *constitutionalization*, or *constitutionalism*, understood as the increasing dominance of constitutional norms to set the terms of political discourse. According to Ran Hirschl, this process amounts to "the wholesale transfer to the courts of some of the most pertinent and polemical political controversies a democratic polity can contemplate",[19] represented by the increasing tendency of states to attach ever-increasing and exercisable "bills of rights" to their constitutions.

Another, less problematizing and more empirically-driven approach to the role of legal rules *viz.* politics is the notion of *legalization*: Kenneth Abbott et al. have suggested that legalization, conceptualized as the sum total of obligation (that actors are bound by a rule or commitment), precision (that the rule or commitment is unambiguously defined) and delegation (that third parties are granted authority to apply the rule), can provide a common ground for political scientists and lawyers in their approaches to international law.[20] Unlike the literature on juridification, in which the general diagnosis seems to be that law is everywhere expanding, the notion of legalization does not necessarily entail increase or decrease in the numbers or ranges of legal rules. Rather, approaching law as a composite of obligation, precision and delegation provides basic tools with which to examine the actors involved in the creation and application of legal rules, which will necessarily vary considerably among different

---

17 Leslie F. Goldstein, 'From Democracy to Juristocracy' (2004) 38 *Law and Society Review* 611.

18 Goldstein 2004, 613.

19 Ran Hirschl, 'The New Constitutionalism and the Judicialization of Pure Politics Worldwide' (2006) 75 *Fordham L. Rev.* 721, 722.

20 Kenneth W. Abbott et al., 'The Concept of Legalization' (2000) 54 *International Organization* 401, 402.

institutions and legal areas. At the high end of the spectrum, where the constituency, rules and institutions entrusted with their interpretation are crystal clear, Abbott et al. localize institutions like the ECtHR and the International Criminal Court. At the low end of the spectrum, they place informal groups like the Group of 7 whose relation to and authority over international legal rules is anything but clear-cut.[21]

We can naturally also find further theories and concepts that seek to capture law's many-sided engagement with and regulation of the social world. In the ambit of this article, however, we want to engage more closely with the "scheme for explanatory reasoning", provided by the five-dimensional model of juridification developed by Blichner and Molander.[22] This model breaks down processes of juridification into (A) constitutive change, (B) the expansion and differentiation of law, (C) increased conflict solving by recourse to law, (D) increased judicial power, and (E) legal framing. The model is clearly derivative of earlier discussions of juridification, summarizing the main positions sketched above. Additionally, however, Blichner and Molander emphasize the often overlooked interrelationships between all the different dimensions, both in general and as they appear in the work of some of the major theorists of juridification, while also adding the notion of "legal framing"—the process by which social actors increasingly see themselves as parts of a common legal order—as a novel item to the analysis of juridification.[23]

Now, in Blichner's and Molander's and also Loick's reading, Habermas' take on juridification is clearly normative, perhaps in a predominantly negative rather than a positive sense. The phrasing "colonization" suggests as much.[24] This also appears to be the case at least as far as the fourth "epochal wave" of juridification, embodied and played out in the democratic welfare state and its policies, is concerned and which, to Habermas' mind, in an ambivalent fashion

---

21 Abbott et al. 2000, 406. The Group of Seven (G7) is an informal bloc of industrialized democracies—Canada, France, Germany, Italy, Japan, the United Kingdom, and the United States—that meets annually to discuss issues such as global economic governance, international security, and energy policy.

22 Blichner and Molander 2008, 37.

23 Blichner and Molander 2008, 47–48.

24 Colonization—the central motor of which to Habermas is law—means that an "autonomous subsystem" imposes its own rationality "into the lifeworld *from outside* … and force a process of assimilation upon it". Habermas 1987, 355; Loick 2014, 759–60. "By the concept of lifeworld, Habermas understands a cluster of implicitly known, pre-reflective, linguistic-cultural traditional norms and values, which sustain the everyday practical communication of individuals." Loick 2014, 759.

circumscribe individual fundamental rights and freedoms.[25] Law as the primary "motor" of colonization both empowers and emancipates those previously disadvantaged, and incapacitates and exerts violence through the very form of its abstract and formalised rationality.[26]

Although the paradigmatic examples used in the literature as evidence of ongoing juridification are contemporary or from our very recent past, it would be too easy to view the processes that one here seeks to capture as simply "modern". Following Loick, we maintain that processes of juridification and de-juridification have shifted back and forth throughout history. Consequently, the urge to speak of "colonization" may from such a long term perspective seem overly zealous. Moreover, and as Loick notes above, we further question the assumption that the "lifeworld" would to all parts be a non-legal sphere.[27]

Admittedly, such an observation is also dependent on what we understand by "law" and what we consider to be the alternative logics around which other discourses organise themselves[28] and whether or not the logic of law by imposing itself on these other discourses and the "lifeworld" will distort these in some fundamental ways and result in important losses of meaning.[29] As Loick puts it when he seeks to capture what he calls "the ambivalence inherent to the politics of juridification":[30] with regard to "social spheres that are pervaded by

---

25 Habermas 1987, 363–67; Blichner and Molander 2008, 50; Loick 2014, 761–62. "[T]he very mean of guaranteeing freedom ... endangers the freedom of the beneficiaries". Habermas 1987, 362; as cited in Loick 2014, 760.

26 Loick 2014, 760–61, in an analysis of Habermas' position.

27 See e.g. Loick 2014, 762.

28 Cf. Niklas Luhmann, whose theory of modern society as "functionally differentiated into autonomous social systems", and of which "law" and "religion" are two, is analysed with respect to its meaningfulness for the study of law and religion, in Russell Sandberg, 'A sociological theory of law and religion' in Frank Cranmer et al. (eds), *The Confluence of Law and Religion: Interdisciplinary Reflections on the Work of Norman Doe* (Cambridge University Press 2016), 66–77. Of special interest in this context is Sandberg's discussion of Luhmann's idea of social systems in relation to "juridification of religion", Sandberg 2016, 73–74. See also e.g. Russell Sandberg, *Law and Religion* (Cambridge University Press 2011) 193–94.

29 For examples of critiques of the inherent limits of e.g. rights vocabulary and risks involved in an over reliance on rights language from within the disciplines of philosophy, law and theology, see e.g. Elizabeth Wolgast, *The Grammar of Justice* (Cornell University Press, 1987), David Kennedy, *The Dark Sides of Virtue: Reassessing International Humanitarianism* (Princeton University Press 2004), and most recently John Milbank, 'Against Human Rights: Liberty in the Western Tradition' (2012) 1 *Oxford Journal of Law and Religion* 203, and Stanley Hauerwas, 'How to Think Theologically about Rights' (2015) 30 *Journal of Law and Religion* 402.

30 Loick 2014, 757.

multiple relations of power and dominance ... the demand for rights and their establishment ... seems to somehow grasp too little, would be inadequate or even counterproductive".[31] Still, it cannot be denied that modern law, including its formulations of rights, has proven itself to be a strong vocabulary which has influenced and moulded the way we think about societal interaction and perceive of matters of justice.

Perhaps what we end up with is something to the effect that has been articulated by Axel Honneth when he posits that law is "the expression of an original social component of human subjectivity".[32] Law both plays and has a role to play in life and human interaction, but it seems hardly adequate for law to embrace or regulate in an absolutist fashion all of reality. On the other hand, what are or should be the limits of law? Again, it comes back to the question of what is "law". In this article, however, our foremost interests are the processes of juridification as such, rather than a normative assessment of these or an assertion of law's correct place and boundaries.

Moreover, the focus of this article is not juridification *as such*, but more specifically the inquiry of whether or not juridification could be a useful conceptual tool in a quest to analyse and understand more profoundly and comprehensively law's engagement and entanglement with religion. Sure enough, in some legal cultures, law is seen—at least ideally—as disinterested with respect to religion and as outside of the phenomenon of religion; religion and law, perhaps in a "Luhmannian way", being perceived of as two separate discourses with few points of contact and entry-points for translation into each other.[33] This is a position that has been challenged from many sides and we encounter today a wide array of scholarly attempts to understand how law engages with and affects religion and vice versa. This does seem to signal something more than simple disinterest, strictly separate sovereignty spheres, or the like. What we come across instead is "intertwinement",[34] or perhaps "confluence",[35] or "dialectical interaction".[36]

---

31 Loick 2014, 758.

32 Honneth's idea as explained by Loick. Loick 2014, 765.

33 For a short analysis of Luhmann's thinking, which is sympathetic to Luhmann's theory and sees various uses for it with regard to the field of law and religion, see Sandberg 2016.

34 Lisbet Christoffersen, 'Intertwinement: A New Concept for Understanding Religion-Law Relations' (2006) 19 *Nordic Journal of Religion and Society* 107.

35 This is the term used in the title of a newly edited volume published to celebrate the 25-year anniversary of the LLM degree in Canon Law at Cardiff University as well as the academic accomplishments in the field of law and religion of Norman Doe. Cranmer et al. (eds) 2016.

36 John Witte Jr., 'The Interdisciplinary Growth of Law and Religion', in Cranmer et al. (eds) 2016, 247.

Importantly, and grounding the development of a multidimensional model, Blichner and Molander dismiss the tendency in parts of the literature to consider any one dimension of juridification as an irreversible, linear process towards the increasing power of law in society, and to see the different dimensions as inextricably linked to one another. More specifically, they suggest two propositions that can be utilized for the operationalization of their model in empirical research: First, links between different dimensions of juridification cannot be assumed, but must be empirically substantiated, as "one type of juridification may gather speed, halt or be turned around without a parallel effect on the others".[37] Second, relationships between different dimensions "may be linked any which way, positively or negatively, meaning that any model must be empirically substantiated".[38] Recognizing that a "likely" model of juridification would be (B → C → D → A) → E, under which legal framing is the end product of a gradual expansion of law's remit that culminates with constitutional amendments, Blichner and Molander suggests a "more dynamic and complex" relationship among the five dimensions, while also recognizing that "[l]acking empirical support it is not possible to say anything about these relationships other than in hypothetical form, and even then it would be difficult to establish any general trends".[39]

To move beyond hypotheticals, we spend part 3 of this article examining the different dimensions suggested by Blichner and Molander, including the potential relationships between the dimensions, taking into account both positive and negative relations, and asking how these different processes have played out in the regulation of religion. More to the point, we will critically interrogate the composition of the dimensions in themselves, seeking to address the specific contextual circumstances represented by religion, as one instance of the "third sector" in Teubner's regulatory trilemma, or one specific dimension of Habermas' notion of the "lifeworld".

2 Unpacking the Relationship between Law and Religion

Despite the large and growing scholarly interest in the study of law and religion, which has recently become "a global brand recognized anywhere in the world",[40] questions concerning the origins, scope and consequences of the

---

37 Blichner and Molander 2008, 49.

38 Blichner and Molander 2008, 49.

39 Blichner and Molander 2008, 49–50.

40 Silvio Ferrari (ed), *Routledge Handbook of Law and Religion* (Routledge 2015) 2.

ongoing growth in the regulation and adjudication of religion have so far not been examined in the research literature, beyond general claims concerning the "resurgence" or "comeback" of religion in the public sphere, and the increased religious diversity of Western societies. Scholars within the field have long relied on conceptions of "law" and "religion" as interrelated dimensions of human living that "exist in all human communities, regardless of time, place and culture".[41] Their broad engagement with law and religion notwithstanding, scholars have so far displayed little interest to move beyond established conceptions of "law" and "religion", leaving these concepts and the modalities of their mutual interactions assumed and undertheorized.

An Empirical and Comparative Approach

One important and influential approach to law's engagement with religion and religion's engagement with law can be found in the writings of Norman Doe. What we encounter here, in the attempt to capture both sides of the equation, is an empirical and comparative approach, not a "theoretical" and "prescriptive" one.[42] Doe has meticulously mapped legislation on law and religious regulation in Europe, systematizing the body of rules and identifying commonalities, on the one hand, in how national, regional and international law regulates and affects religion—something which he calls "religion law" or "law on religion"[43]—and, on the other hand, in what he calls (internal) "religious law", an admittedly broad category in this context.[44] Doe also uses "juridical instruments" and "regulatory instruments" when talking about the "variety of normative or prescriptive entities" that within faith communities "contain rules of conduct",[45] and which depending on the precise faith community may well include regulation of both local, regional, national and international reach.[46]

41 John Witte, Jr., 'Law, Religion, and Human Rights' (1996) 28 *Columbia Human Rights Law Review* 1, 3.

42 Mark Hill, 'Renaissance and Re-engagement: Norman Doe's Achievement in the Discipline of Law and Religion', in Cranmer et al. (eds) 2016, 1–15, 8.

43 Norman Doe, *Law and Religion in Europe: A Comparative Introduction* (Oxford University Press 2011).

44 Norman Doe, *Christian Law: Contemporary Principles* (Cambridge University Press 2013) 11. For a short definition of "religion law" and "religious law", see e.g. also Norman Doe and Russell Sandberg, 'Introduction' in Norman Doe & Russell Sandberg (eds), *Law and Religion: New Horizons* (Peeters 2010) 9–12, 11.

45 Doe 2013, 5.

46 Doe 2013, 19–29.

As Mark Hill has recently characterized this work as far as its methodology goes, both with regard to what could be called "comparative religious law"[47] and "religion law",[48] (and Doe agrees to its application to both "religious" and "secular" law):[49]

> [it is] neither prescriptive nor theoretical. Instead, and with a beguiling but painstaking simplicity, Doe lays side by side the source materials of the laws and compares their provisions on a subject-by-subject basis.[50] ... Doe's work is characterised by dense referencing indicating from where each component statement of law or practice has been derived, a clear narrative pulling together all the seemingly disparate strands and then the distillation of the accumulated knowledge into a series of principles (often with derivative micro-principles) which can then be road-tested to ensure that in the process of reduction they remain vital and relevant to each of the Churches studied.[51]

What we find in the scholarly work of Doe is then not only—or even primarily perhaps—a study of "secular" law's engagement with religion, but also an important take on law as "religion", or perhaps more to the point, as "religious".

While critics drawing on the works of Talal Asad and others have targeted the supposedly secular nature of law and the adverse effects of this "blessed ignorance" (see below),[52] much of law today is, of course, anything if not also explicit about its religious and theological sources of inspiration, be it in the area of family law, finance law, criminal law, or the like. And as John Witte Jr. points out in an article that offers an overview of the interdisciplinary field of law and religion research, the input does not simply come in the form of historic remnants, it is also a present-day phenomenon all over the world:

---

47 Hill 2016, 8, 13; see e.g. Doe 2013.

48 Hill, 2016, 9–10; Doe 2011, 1.

49 Doe 2013, 6 (fn. 29); referring to his books *Canon Law in the Anglican Communion: A Worldwide Perspective* (Clarendon Press 1998), and *Law and Religion in Europe: A Comparative Introduction* (Oxford University Press 2011).

50 Hill 2016, 8.

51 Hill 2016, 8–9.

52 See e.g. Talal Asad, *Formations of the Secular: Christianity, Islam, Modernity* (Stanford University Press 2003).

> [A] small library of books has also emerged ... documenting the contributions of the world's religions and their religious legal systems to the secular legal systems around them, both historically and currently. Part of this inquiry concerns the exportation, transplantation or accommodation of discrete internal religious rules or procedures into secular legal systems. But more of this inquiry concerns the influence of religious ideas and practices on the complex doctrines of the public, private, penal and procedural law of the State.[53]

Put in another way, the object of study and systematization for Doe, and others following in his wake,[54] is both the relations of religious communities with each other and between religious communities and the state and wider society,[55] and the internal structuring and governance of the life of religious institutions on the basis of their self-understanding and in response to laws on religion; both "external" and "internal" relations, both "external" and "internal" rules governing religion.

Hence, "religion" is not per se the space of the non-legal. Instead, religion takes juridical form. There is a link between faith and form, the overall purpose often enough being to provide order and facilitate mission.[56] Doe talks of religious law as "applied theology", at least in a general sense even if it may not apply to every single little rule.[57] Given all this, what we encounter is a comprehensive study of constitutional arrangements and establishment of religion, of concrete "secular" legislation and religious regulation, of questions of authority, jurisdiction and governance, a study of institutions, both religious and nonreligious, and of the kinds of legal persons that religious communities are conceptualised as. There is less of a focus on religious individuals and their legal framing than on institutional religion. Less attention also seems to be given to concrete adjudicative processes and dispute resolution with reference

53 Witte 2016, 256.

54 Worth mentioning here is, for example, as Doe also does, the many volumes from the annual proceedings that come out of the European Consortium for Church and State Research. As such, the individual contributions to those edited volumes may not take a comparative approach (Doe 2011, 4), but as a whole, the edited proceedings address a common theme and survey national approaches to this topic through case studies of many European countries.

55 See e.g. Doe 2013, 274–309, 346–83.

56 See e.g. Doe 2013, 29–33.

57 Doe 2013, 384–85, in the context of talking of the laws of churches.

to law, and to other forms of "law in action". At least Doe concedes as much both with regard to "religious law"[58] and "religion law"[59].[60]

Moreover, Doe also notes that in his work on religion law in Europe, he does not situate national laws on religion in a political context. This, he argues, would demand a historical outlook with a focus on legislative processes and the debates related to these.[61] Thus, while the work of Doe is profoundly empirical as far as the object of study goes, it shows clear overlaps with the matters that Blichner and Molander single out for study, and the two approaches converge in the focus on law from both an external perspective and from the perspective of "internal self-description".[62] However, Doe's perspective also differs from Blichner and Molander's model given its in-depth focus on *non-state* law and what Doe titles "quasi-legislation",[63] and consequently also in this respect the relations *between* different regulatory systems. Although, admittedly, Blichner and Molander's focus on processes of juridification and de-juridification to a

58 See e.g. Doe 2013, 387: "[F]urther study is needed on the application of laws ... such as the enforcement of spiritual sanctions ... The same applies to difficulties associated with the administration of laws...". Although see also e.g. the collaborative work of Doe in the area of religious family law and the publications coming out of the project 'Social Cohesion and Civil Law: Marriage, Divorce and Religious Courts', <http://www.law.cf.ac.uk/clr/research/cohesion.html> accessed 7 October 2016: Rt Hon Lord Justice McFarlane, '"Am I Bothered?" The Relevance of Religious Courts to a Civil Judge' (2011) 41 *Family Law* 946; Gillian Douglas et al., 'Marriage and Divorce in Religious Courts: A Case Study' (2011) 41 *Family Law* 956; Gillian Douglas et al., 'The Role of Religious Tribunals in Regulating Marriage and Divorce' (2012) 24 *Child and Family Law Quarterly* 139–57; Gillian Douglas et al., 'Accommodating Religious Divorce in the Secular State: A Case-Study Analysis' in Mavis Maclean and John Eekelaar (eds), *Families: Deviance, Diversity and the Law* (Hart Publishing 2013) 185–201; Russell Sandberg et al., 'Britain's Religious Tribunals: "Joint Governance" in Practice' (2013) 33 *Oxford Journal of Legal Studies* 263.

59 Doe 2011, 261. The same goes for matters of legal framing. "Empirical research would be invaluable to uncover the practical difficulties which, for example, religious groups face in seeking legal personality ... Related to this is the need for a general religious perspective on national laws and the issues they address." Doe 2011, 261.

60 Doe has called for a "sociology of law on religion" (Hill 2016, 11; Norman Doe, 'A Sociology of Law on Religion—Towards a New Discipline: Legal Responses to Religious Pluralism in Europe' (2004) *Law & Justice* 152, 268), observing that sociology of religion can offer "fundamental propositions about the contemporary role of religion in society" which "may be used to understand religion law more deeply in its social context". Doe 2011, 260.

61 Doe 2011, 261.

62 Terminology borrowed from Sandberg 2016, 67.

63 See e.g. Doe 2013, 11.

certain extent allows for exactly this kind of inquiry, as does their focus on conflict resolution and legal framing of individuals and collectives.

The Critical Approach

Another strand in the literature on law and religion takes a more critical approach to the nature and effects of legal regulations,[64] and has also encountered its own vocal critics.[65] These scholars offer a postcolonial and deconstructivist reading of modern "liberal" and "secular" law, unveiling its religious prejudices and political inclinations and the normative commitments of the legal framework. They draw attention to categories, concepts and ideas that are crucial to legal formulations of rights and freedoms in regard to religion and that structure adjudication in religious matters. Furthermore, they trace the historical development of these categories, concepts and ideas—including also the idea of law as "secular"—finding that what we encounter at the root of it all seems akin to a particular Western Protestant understanding of what faith is and should be all about.[66] However, they also revisit and revise this particular narrative in part by tracing the "multiple histories and genealogies" of the concept of religious freedom across the globe.[67]

---

64 See e.g. Nehal Bhuta, 'Two Concepts of Religious Freedom in the European Court of Human Rights' (2014) 113 *South Asian Quarterly* 9–35; Peter G. Danchin, 'Religious Freedom in the Panopticon of Enlightenment Rationality', in Winnifred F. Sullivan et al. (eds), *Politics of Religious Freedom* (University of Chicago Press 2015) 240–52; Elizabeth Shakman Hurd, *Beyond Religious Freedom: The New Global Politics of Religion* (Princeton University Press 2015); Saba Mahmood, *Religious Difference in A Secular Age: A Minority Report* (Princeton University Press 2016); Winnifred F. Sullivan, *The Impossibility of Religious Freedom* (Princeton University Press 2007); Winnifred F. Sullivan et al. (eds), *Politics of Religious Freedom* (University of Chicago Press 2015).

65 See e.g. David Little, 'Human Rights, Religious Freedom, and Peace', Keynote address delivered keynote address at the 22nd Annual BYU Symposium on Religion and International Law, 4 October 2015, <https://www.iclrs.org/content/blurb/files/David%20Little%20Keynote%20Address%202015.pdf> accessed 13 June 2017.

66 See e.g., Peter G. Danchin, 'The Emergence and Structure of Religious Freedom in International Law Reconsidered' (2007/2008) 23 *Journal of Law and Religion* 455; Pamela Slotte, 'The Religious and the Secular in European Human Rights Discourse' (2012 (2010)) 21 *Finnish Yearbook of International Law* 231, as well as the various contributions in Part I of Winnifred F. Sullivan, Robert A. Yelle and Mateo Taussig-Rubbo, *After Secular Law* (Stanford University Press 2011), and Robert Yelle, 'Imagining the Hebrew Republic: Christian Genealogies of Religious Freedom', in Sullivan et al. (eds) 2015, 17–28.

67 Winnifred F. Sullivan et al., 'Introduction' in Sullivan et al. (eds) 2015, 1–9, 5–7. See also the various other contributions to Sullivan et al. (eds) 2015.

The underlying premise of this criticism is that "legal religion" is unable to truly capture "lived religion",[68] or the "lived realities of religious experience".[69] This depiction of law and its preferences for specific forms of religion could easily be read as very much of a colonization of lifeworlds, indeed perhaps something coming close to a distortion of religious lifeworlds. If the critique is to be believed, it seems to require that those who seek legal recognition have no choice but to re-describe, "reframe", their religious identities in the most drastic of fashions, provided that they do not in the first place fall within the category of liberal protestant faith—or indeed other conceptions of religion—that the legal framework has been moulded around.

Hence, if anything, what we encounter here is a strong normative denunciation of juridification in matters of religion: "To continue to use the word [religion] in law is to invite discrimination."[70] However, proponents of this line of critique also stress that:

> Our project does not take a position for or against religious freedom. Rather, we are interested in laying out the kind of work that advocacy for religious freedom has done and is doing in various times and places, and the kind of political and legal worlds it has created and is creating. Our basic assumption is that, before either championing religious freedom or rejecting it, we need to understand the complex social and legal lives of this concept.[71]

An objection against this "critical" approach is that—opposite to what the quote leads us to believe—they become highly theoretical, discursively analytical and too fixated on the legal texts themselves that articulate, for example, a legal right to freedom of religion or belief. It is not that their critique of the failures of law to address matters of faith would not in part be persuasive and hit the mark. But as a consequence of the simultaneously limited focus of their analysis—more on law "on the books" than law "in action"[72]—they can end up offering reductive readings of what actually happens "on the ground" when

68 See e.g. Sullivan et al. 2015, 7.

69 Elizabeth Shakman Hurd, 'Believing in Religious Freedom' in Sullivan et al. (eds) 2015, 45–56, 47.

70 Sullivan et al. 2015, 7. The word used in this context by the authors is actually "legalization of religion". Sullivan et al. 2015, 8.

71 Sullivan et al. 2015, 2.

72 Cf. John Witte, Jr. and John A. Nichols, '"Come Now Let Us Reason Together": Restoring Religious Freedom in America and Abroad' (2017) 92 *Notre Dame Law Review* 427, 436.

matters of religion are negotiated through law.[73] And an in-depth, comprehensive and contextual understanding of the purposes, issues and perspectives that are afforded significance in adjudication processes and decision-making in individual cases would be key so as to—in the words of Jason A. Springs—counteract "excessive discursive analytical tendencies".[74]

Translated into the terms of juridification, the critical position overlooks, if not altogether, at least a substantive part of the multidimensional processes affecting law's engagement with religion and the involved agents and institutions.[75] In fact, this resembles a critical remark that Loick directs to Habermas.[76] Hence, while seeking to expose the "politics" of law with regard to religion, that unveiling, commendable as it is, does not in fact go far enough.[77]

Disaggregating Law and Religion

There are of course also other more theoretical or philosophically oriented ways to analyse law's engagement with religion. They may or may not also end up finding that the legal framework is sufficient or inadequate; that religion deserves being singled out for special legal protection, or not. One such perspective has been put forward by Cécile Laborde. In common with scholars

73 Jason A. Springs, 'Tentacles of the Leviathan? Nationalism, Islamophobia, and the Insufficiency-yet-Indispensability of Human Rights for Religious Freedom in Contemporary Europe' (2016) 84 *Journal of the American Academy of Religion* 903. However, see also Sullivan et al. 2015, for a discussion that implicitly counters exactly this critique: "The present volume [shows] ..., through the work of various scholars working in a variety of geographical regions, that the meaning and practice of a right to religious liberty varies and shifts depending on the particular configuration of state-religion accommodation and the impact of other historical and transnational forces. Far from being able to be reduced to a question of compliance or noncompliance with a stable, uncontested norm that is being progressively disseminated globally (despite occasional setbacks), promoting a right to religious freedom shapes political and religious possibilities in particular ways, though always differently in different contexts." Sullivan et al. 2015, 9.

74 Springs 2016, 3. See also Springs 2016, 4.

75 For example, in Winnifred Fallers Sullivan's work, we find a more multidimensional focus that includes also, for example, matters relevant to studies of what we term here "constitutional juridification and religion", namely issues of establishment and disestablishment of religion. Winnifred Fallers Sullivan and Lori G. Beaman (eds), *Varieties of Religious Establishment* (Ashgate 2013).

76 Loick 2014, 762.

77 This is a critique that the authors of the present article take to heart, given the affinity that we in various writings have shown with scholars seeking to expose the "politics of law". See e.g. Slotte 2012, and Helge Årsheim, *Lost in Translation? Religion-Making at Four UN Human Rights Committees, 1993–2013*, Ph.D. dissertation (Akademika 2015).

presented above, she critically investigates legal constructions of religion. Her primary interest is not to describe all the possible ways in which law may engage with religion. What she does is, rather, to narrow in on what *could* adequately be law's task in relation to religion, echoing hereby the assertion above that not all of social reality can meaningfully be given legal articulation.

> … not all values can, or indeed should, be expressed by the law. Just as we would not want the law to express the whole of the value of 'the family', for example, so we would not want the law to capture of the whole of the value of religion. At best, the law will put forward an interpretive notion of 'the family', or of religion. That a particular law or theory does not capture what religion really is, therefore, is not, in itself, a sufficient objection to it. What matters is that the law, or the theory, expresses and protects the correct underlying values.[78]

Hence, Laborde's project is normative. She is in search of an "inclusive approach to religious freedom",[79] which would be able to rebut the kinds of criticisms against exclusivity/reductionism, particularism and discrimination that we saw that the previously mentioned critics have directed against "legal religion".[80]

Laborde finds that the special legally entrenched right to religious freedom could be "disaggregated". The reason is that the purpose for law's engagement with religion, as far as protection of matters of faith—and the various underlying "legally relevant normative values"[81] or "goods" that are at play here[82]—is concerned, could be adequately captured through other generic "liberal rights", such as freedom of thought, freedom of association and freedom of expression: "The starting point of the disaggregation strategy is to suggest that different parts of the law should capture different dimensions of religion for the protection of different normative values."[83] Aside from staying more

78 Cécile Laborde, 'Religion in the Law: The Disaggregation Approach' (2015), 2. <https://raptconference.files.wordpress.com/2015/04/laborde.pdf> accessed 13 June 2017.

79 Laborde 2015, 2.

80 For Laborde's analysis of these critiques, see Laborde 2015, 3–5.

81 Laborde 2015, 11.

82 See Laborde 2015, 9, for a short explanation of her understanding of "good" in this context.

83 Laborde 2015, 11, who puts forward this "non-exhaustive list of legally relevant dimensions of religion": "1. Religion as a conception of the good life; 2. Religion as conscientious moral obligation; 3. Religion as key feature of identity; 4. Religion as mode of human association; 5. Religion as vulnerability class; 6. Religion as totalizing institution; 7. Religion as inaccessible doctrine".

attuned to all the various forms that individual and collective religious life might take, this would also in more adequate fashion place religious and non-religious persons and groups on an equal footing.

In sum, a survey of different scholarly perspectives on the entanglement of law with religion show both disparities and resemblances amongst each other and in relation to the approach to the phenomenon of juridification. It seems that in relation to these other outlooks, Blichner and Molander suggest to us a perspective that incorporates an inquiry into the theoretical and the empirical, into the legal and the political, and a multidimensional focus on processes and texts, actors and institutions. The other scholarly perspectives, from their particular angles, may give valuable contributions as we in the following analyse in more detail the five different dimensions/processes of juridification (and de-juridification) with regard to religion.

3 From Law and Religion to the Juridification of Religion

In this section, we explore the utility of the multidimensional model of juridification suggested by Blichner and Molander for the study of law and religion. As discussed in the previous section, the interrelationship between law and religion spreads out across a number of different subthemes that need to be addressed both separately and in conjunction in order to examine the ways and the extent to which the regulation of religion is affected by or entangled with the overarching process of juridification or indeed also de-juridification.

3A *Constitutional Change*

> According to the first definition juridification is a process where norms constitutive for a political order are established or changed to the effect of adding to the competencies of the legal system. Roughly one may distinguish between constitutive norms concerning procedures, the acceptable uses of state power and the separation of powers.[84]

To Blichner and Molander, this dimension of juridification has two facets: the establishment of a legal order as such (A1)—also identified in the literature as a case of "legalization"—and the establishment and the articulation of constitutional norms both within and without formal constitutions (A2).[85] Under

84 Blichner and Molander 2008, 39.
85 Blichner and Molander 2008, 39.

juridification A1, constitutions structure how power is to be shared and limited; they authorize the power to make decisions in society and the power to execute these decisions. Constitutions have also become a place to articulate core fundamental rights and freedoms.[86] However, Blichner and Molander also attribute these authorizations to juridification A2, which comprises constitutive norms in the form of legal doctrines, "legal or jurisprudential regimes or legal paradigms, to mention some of the concepts used to depict relatively stable systemic fundamentals that structure legal decision making." When, for example, legal doctrines are "formally constitutionalised", we see instances of a merger of A1 and A2. However, Blichner and Molander only consider this move part of juridification A in so far as it to some extent grounds "the competencies of the legal system".[87]

Constitutive Juridifications of Religion

It goes without saying that many different aspects of law are attributed to the constitutional dimension of juridification and that we are not able to explore here all their entanglements with religion. Blichner and Molander are seeking to pinpoint *fundamental* aspects of legal systems; the premises for the legal practice as a whole and the parameters within which legal discourse is carried out. Clearly, non-legal ideas and concepts play a crucial role here. A considerable amount of ink has also been spilt lately on tracing the genealogy of foundational legal and political concepts, including their supposedly religious roots.[88]

What is clear is that there can be hardly a more classical case to take as an example for exploring the juridification or indeed the de-juridification of religion, than the issue of the placement of religion in the establishment of a legal order (A1). That this is a pressing and contentious matter and has been so throughout much of history also goes without saying. As formulated by James Madison in 1803: "The purpose of separation of church and state is to keep forever from these shores the ceaseless strife that has soaked the soil of Europe in blood for centuries."[89]

---

86 See e.g. Gerhard Robbers, 'Church and State Relations in the Constitutions' in W. Cole Durham, Jr. et al. (eds), *Law, Religion, Constitution: Freedom of Religion, Equal Treatment, and the Law* (Ashgate 2013) 58–60.

87 Blichner and Molander 2008, 40.

88 See e.g. the references mentioned in part 2 above which surveys law & religion research.

89 [Letter objecting to the use of government land for churches, 1803]", James Madison.

Since the early rise of constitutionalism in the late 18th century, religion has been a central component of constitutive juridification. Religion has frequently been shuffled around in domestic constitutions following regime change,[90] including during processes of decolonization that may also transfer and institutionalise colonial imaginations and practices.[91] Likewise, the changed international relations and obligations of a state may trigger constitutional reform through the increased recognition of human rights at the constitutional level, as has been the case for many European states acceding to the Council of Europe and its European Convention of Human Rights and Fundamental Freedoms (ECHR, 1950), and to the European Union (EU).

Religion was also a battleground issue during the negotiations towards a constitution for the EU: The attempt to introduce into the preambles of the Constitutional and Lisbon Treaties of the EU references to God and the continent's Christian heritage was controversial from the start and eventually failed. Of course, this notwithstanding, religion still plays a significant role in the European integration project.[92] While state-religion matters are primarily viewed as matters falling within the competence of the member states, the EU in various ways has regulated its relation to, interacts and cooperates with religion and adjudicates in religious matters.[93] What is more, the role of religion in the negotiations leading up to the adoption of the Universal Declaration of Human Rights (UDHR, 1948) and the ECHR is currently being unearthed by a new generation of human rights scholars and historians.[94]

---

90 Jonathan Fox, 'Separation of Religion and State and Secularism in Theory and Practice' (2011) 39 *Religion, State and Society* 384. See also e.g. the various contributions in Alessandro Ferrari and James Toronto (eds), *Religions and Constitutional Transitions in the Muslim Mediterranean: The Pluralistic Moment*, ICLARS Series on Law and Religion (Routledge 2017).

91 See e.g. Mahmood 2016.

92 Lucian Leustean and John Madeley, 'Religion, Politics and Law in the European Union: An Introduction' (2009) 37 *Religion, State and Society* 3.

93 See e.g. Ronan McCrea, *Religion and the Public Order of the European Union* (Oxford University Press 2010); Doe 2011. Here, Ronan McCrea has underscored that the religious/ Christian and humanist heritages through their determining and partly conflicting notions *de facto* continue to have a bearing in a way that is not in all parts favourable to "outsider faiths". See e.g. McCrea 2010, 4–15, where he observes that religion is chiefly seen as a matter of choice and is linked to individual and collective identity and culture. Truth claims are belittled and confined to the private sphere.

94 Linde Lindkvist, 'The Politics of Article 18: Religious Liberty in the Universal Declaration of Human Rights' (2013) 4 *Humanity: An International Journal of Human Rights,*

Constitutions have featured provisions on the regulation of individual and collective religious issues since the late 18th century, with the French and US constitutions serving as templates for a wave of European and Latin American constitutions in the 19th century, and indeed later on too.[95] However, different states negotiate their relation to religion in different ways, including at the level of constitutions. A common means to roughly categorise the overall types of state-religion relations is to distinguish between those states which have an established religion in the form of, for instance, a national or folk church; those which, while basically endorsing separation, cooperate with religion in various ways and may have settled this formally in, for instance, treaties; and those that at an official symbolic level attempt to disassociate themselves from religion.[96] This will be reflected most typically in the constitutions of countries, and periods of constitutional change and the deliberations that accompany the drafting of constitutional amendments offer insights into how state-religion

---

Humanitarianism, and Development 429; Bhuta 2014; Samuel Moyn, 'From Communist to Muslim: European Human Rights, the Cold War, and Religious Liberty' 2014 (113) *South Atlantic Quarterly* 63; Pamela Slotte, '"Blessed are the Peacemakers": Christian Internationalism, Ecumenical Voices and the Universal Declaration of Human Rights' in Pamela Slotte and Miia Halme-Tuomisaari (eds), *Revisiting the Origins of Human Rights* (Cambridge University Press 2015) 293–329; Marco Duranti, *The Conservative Human Rights Revolution: European Identity, Transnational Politics, and the Origins of the European Convention* (Oxford University Press 2017); Linde Lindkvist, *Religious Freedom and the Universal Declaration of Human Rights* (Cambridge University Press 2017).

Whether a "constitutionalisation" of international law as such (and/or particular functional regimes within it) has or should take place, or whether what we have been witnessing over the years is instead "fragmentation"—or indeed both—is a much debated question with strong voices both pro and contra. For overviews, see e.g. Rossana Deplano, 'Fragmentation and Constitutionalisation of International Law: A Theoretical Inquiry' (2013) 6 *European Journal of Legal Studies* 67; Andrzej Jakubowski and Karolina Wierczyńska (eds), *Fragmentation vs the Constitutionalisation of International Law: A Practical Inquiry* (Routledge 2016); as well as importantly International Law Commission, 'Fragmentation of International Law: Difficulties Arising from the Diversification and Expansion of International Law' (13 April 2006) UN Doc A/CN.4/L.682. Likewise, scholars differ as to whether what we are witnessing within e.g. the European human rights system could be conceptualised in terms of constitutionalisation, with the ECtHR functioning as a constitutional court, or not. Also here different normative standpoints abound.

95 Jeroen Temperman, *State-Religion Relationships and Human Rights Law: Towards a Right to Religiously Neutral Governance*, Studies in Religion, Secular Beliefs and Human Rights, vol. 8 (Martinus Nijhoff Publishers 2010), 118–19, with regard to the migration of the US constitutional clause on non-establishment.

96 See e.g. Doe 2011, 2, 5.

relations are conceptualised and normatively understood. The arrangements tell us something as regards divisions of authority and spheres of governance. They are sites for core national concepts and expose ideas about, for instance, citizenship as is apparent from current securitization discourses in many countries that call for a renegotiation or reinterpretation of constitutionally enshrined religious rights and the legitimate place of religion in societal life.[97]

In his book *Law and Religion in Europe*, Norman Doe offers a useful overview of current constitutional and other legal arrangements in European states. Jonathan Fox's *A World Survey of Religion and the State* likewise provides an overview but this time with a global reach of, among other things, what he titles "structural changes in the relationship between religion and state" and which take place, for example, at the level of constitutions when the official relation of a state to religion is re-negotiated.[98] In turn, *Constitutions and Religious Freedom* by Frank B. Cross, a more theoretically geared account perhaps, narrows in on constitutional protection of individual and collective religious freedoms and questions the sensibleness and necessity of legally privileging religion in this manner. While theoretically global in scope, much of the in-depth empirical discussion focuses on the US.

These overviews are exactly that: overviews. They may be detailed enough in the comparative material that they compile, but as Cross himself notes in relation to systems of measuring religious freedom world-wide like the *Pew Forum*, the *Religion and State* (RAS), *Restrictions on Religious Freedom* (RFF) and *Association of Religion Data Archives* (ARDA): within the classifications of states, there may be important factual differences that go unnoticed. Sometimes the results may even end up looking outright curious. Moreover, measuring systems like the ones mentioned differ somewhat in terms of what they set out to measure. In addition it will often enough be difficult to deduce anything about the practical effect of the constitutional provisions accounted for, including the influence they assert on the broader legal culture.[99] As Souad Ghaouti-Malki points out with regard to Algerian constitutions from 1962 onwards: "All drafters of Algerian constitutions have managed to 'expertly' inject doses of religion into them, doing so in such a way that these appear to be

97 For the last remark, see e.g. Alessandro Ferrari, 'Dynamics of Religious Freedom on the Two Mediterranean Sides: An Interconnected History' in Ferrari and Toronto (eds) 2017, 5–6.

98 Jonathan Fox, *A World Survey of Religion and the State* (Cambridge University Press 2008) 77.

99 Frank B. Cross, *Constitutions and Religious Freedom* (Cambridge University Press 2015) 69–70, 75–77. See also Temperman 2010, 35.

above the state institutions, interfering very rarely with the juridical norms."[100] According to Cross, a constitution "may be simply aspirational, setting out the nation's ideals, with little expectation they would be put into practice", for example, or "be adopted for symbolic purposes, to raise a nation's stature or respect in the world community or perhaps to attract foreign capital".[101] This, in effect, is also a reason for stressing the need to empirically explore simultaneously different dimensions of juridification and their interfaces as suggested by Blichner and Molander.

Still, given these caveats, the overviews tell us something about the "precommitments", to use a term adopted by Cross to capture the role of constitutions and particularly of bills of rights as laying down ground rules for governance,[102] about societal spaces that religion is assigned, the ways in which it is allowed legitimately to exercise power, and the social and political functions the state sees fit to allow it.[103]

A survey of the above and other literature shows that different overviews group countries in somewhat different ways. Cross, for example, classifies countries—or "codes constitutions"—by reference, among other things, to the RAS measure system developed by Fox and to Tom Ginsburg's and Zachary Elkins' comprehensive survey of both past and present constitutions of almost all nations.[104] He points out that there are "three primary types of constitutional provisions relevant to religious freedom: (i) provisions creating or banning a state religion; (ii) provisions prohibiting the establishment of religion or

---

100 Souad Ghaouti-Malki, 'The Treatment of the Relationship between Islam and the State in the Algerian Fundamental Texts from 1962 To 2012' in Ferrari and Toronto (eds) 2017, 168.

101 Cross 2015, 107; referring to David S. Law, 'Constitutions' in Peter Cane and Herbert Kritzer (eds), *The Oxford Handbook of Empirical Legal Research* (Oxford University Press 2010).

102 Cross 2015, 110–11.

103 They may pay less attention to the underlying reasons for each constitutional arrangement, which surely reflect a number of concerns and ideas. For a discussion, see e.g. Cross 2015, 5–15. For example, according to Cross, the reasons of constitutional protection may historically have been largely pragmatic—to counteract strife, persecution and unrest and promote societal peace—rather than primarily based on some innate appreciation of religion. Cross 2015, 5–8. Furthermore, looking at societal factors and basing himself on other research and surveys, Cross concludes that: "Democracy appears to promote religious freedom ... a greater Islamic population appears to lead to a tendency to restrict religious freedom. The effects of the rule of law and national wealth are not so clear, though, on a theoretical level." Cross 2015, 100. See also, Cross 2015, 101–104. Cross concludes that the "different societal factors may operate differently, under different constitutional settings". Cross 2015, 104.

104 Zachary Elkins, Tom Ginsbury, and James Melton, *The Endurance of National Constitutions* (Cambridge University Press 2009); Cross 2015, 158.

calling for separation of church and state; and (iii) provisions guaranteeing individuals freedom of religious belief."[105] In Cross' sample, 39% of nations had establishment clauses, over 94% had what he calls free exercise clauses, 21% had a so-called constitutional national religion whereas 23% forbade such. In about 55% of the countries, the matter of national religion was left to other legislation.[106]

For sure, the meaning of a state or national religion may differ and the constitutional protection may serve a symbolic role only. A religion may hold a strong position in society independently of the lack of constitutional status or be established legislatively as a national religion at another legal level.[107] Fox seconds this idea, that in practice, having an official religion can mean many different things in different countries and impact, for example, religious minority positions very differently.[108] Yet, working on the basis of his three basic types, Cross concludes that most constitutions in the world have incorporated provisions aimed at protecting religious freedom, although the particular scope of these differ. Religious freedom is seldom understood as an absolute right, but instead qualified in various ways. This, of course, is also the case with articles protecting freedom of religion or belief at the levels of the UN and regional human rights systems,[109] which also since the mid-20th century have served as inspiration and source for the drafting of new constitutions. This links in with the discussion about legal transplants (or which term one chooses to employ) and how they work as so-called irritants, which is explored in some depth in section 3B below.[110]

According to Cross, few states have the kind of establishment clause that orders the strict separation of religion and state that we find in the US Constitution. As an example he mentions Albania. However, he also refers in this context to Georgia and Argentina, both of which still expressly acknowledge the role of their "historical" religion, and in the case of Argentina even maintains that the state "supports the Roman Catholic Apostolic Religion". From this Cross concludes that the "relative significance of the different

105 Cross 2015, 27.
106 Cross 2015, 161, 164, 166.
107 Cross 2015, 159.
108 Fox 2008, 40.
109 Cross 2015, 154–55.
110 A comprehensive analysis to this effect is Jeroen Temperman's *State-Religion Relationships and Human Rights law*, a normative study of how different state-religion arrangements comply with international human rights law. Temperman 2010.

wording is uncertain, but all reflect a relative commitment to an establishment clause-like protection (or not)".[111]

For reasons of clarity, it would perhaps be better to contend that some constitutions articulate a principle of strict separation of religion and state, whereas others give voice to various levels of recognition, or with Jeroen Temperman's words, "modes of state-religion identification",[112] where he echoes W. Cole Durham.[113] To different degrees states may, for example, support, acknowledge and endorse religion in general, one in particular or several different faiths. They may accommodate religions or lean towards forms of non-identification that still do not amount to strict separation.[114] In fact, it seems reasonable to maintain that various degrees of establishment, broadly conceived, are the rule.[115] National constitutions may expressly recognize the existence of a state religion, as in the case of Denmark with Lutheranism,[116] but the allusions to a higher being or deity may also be more generic, as in the case of Fiji: "worship and reverence to God are the source of good governance".[117] What is recognized is the role of faith as an important normative commitment.

What we find across the world are multi-tiered systems of legal status recognition of religions and beliefs, with different aggregates of legal rights and freedoms.[118] In a terminology that signals a normative stance, Fox talks of "official restrictions" when governments in this and other ways treat different religions differently.[119] Also otherwise, it is clear that scholars hold different

111 Cross 2015, 156.

112 Temperman 2010, 4.

113 W. Cole Durham, 'Perspectives on Religious Liberty: A Comparative Framework' in Johan D. van der Vyver and John Witte, Jr. (eds), *Religious Human Rights in Global Perspective: Legal Perspectives* (Martinus Nijhoff Publishers 1996) 1–44.

114 Temperman 2010, 65–110.

115 For example, Doe asserts that, in effect, the most common model of state-religion relations in Europe, provided that we look beyond the constitutional level, is that of cooperation. Doe 2011, 2.

116 See also e.g. Cross 2015, 156.

117 Cross 2015, 157. See also e.g. Temperman 2010, 77–83; Iván C. Ibán, 'God in Constitutions and Godless Constitutions' in Durham et al. (eds) 2013, 37–55. Importantly, Cross points out a potential problem with such references: "Arjomand (2003) suggests that such provisions may be used to counteract the protection of religious freedom via the constitution or even perhaps through democratic measures." Cross 2015, 157; Said Amir Arjomand, 'Law, Political Reconstruction, and Constitutional Politics' (2003) 18 *International Sociology* 7. For sure, they may be used to destabilise a right to freedom from religion in its various dimensions.

118 Cross 2015, 49–53.

119 Fox 2008, 5.

opinions as to how "state" and "religion" should relate to each other. However, that the position of a religion or belief within national multi-tiered systems of legal recognition differs depending on the nation and region comes as no surprise. Alongside other more or less laudable reasons, it reflects the relative historical and contemporary standing within the society in question.[120]

Temperman (2010) arranges his analysis of constitutive juridification of religion across the world in accordance with types of state-religion arrangements. Fox (2008), in turn, offers an insight into concrete regional differences when it comes to the question of whether a state has an "official religion" and "the extent of government regulation of the majority religion or all religions", which Fox calls "religious regulation" but which we in this article title "religion law". In addition, Fox also surveys "the extent to which the government legislates various aspects of religious law", something which he calls "religious legislation".[121] What he attributes to this category is, however, a broad category of laws that may or may not easily fall into the category of religious law as understood by other scholars. Fox includes both legislation "about religious precepts" and legislation that "supports religion" in this category.[122] An example of the latter could be the subcategory of "fund religious charitable organisations", while "dietary laws", "laws of inheritance defined by religion" or laws that prescribe that businesses should be closed on the Sabbath, for instance, seem more clear cases of juridification of religious law per se.[123] In general, the categories of Fox with their broad area echo the growth of legal regulations of religion as discussed in part 3B.

Regional Tendencies in Constitutive Juridification of Religion

In the period surveyed in his book, the years 1990–2002, Fox detects a general rise in "government involvement with religion" (GIR), especially in terms of support to religion, but also in terms of religious legislation albeit this varies from country to country and type of religious legislation.[124] Also in terms

120 For an overview of what could form background motivations for particular religion-state patterns, see Fox 2008, 353–56.

121 Fox 2008, 5–6. (For comparison, in Fox 2011, he limits religious regulation to "types of restrictions or regulation that can be placed on the majority in a state". Fox 2011, 388.) To be kept in mind is that Fox's analysis here builds on the RAS data covering the period of 1990–2002 and 175 governments (with effective control over a particular territory.) Fox 2008, 7–8, 47–48.

122 Fox 2011, 388, where he accounts for the categories used in his 2008 study.

123 See e.g. Fox 2008, 321.

124 Fox 2008, 6, 8.

of religious regulation he detects a general rise, the same caveats applying.[125] Hence, juridification of religion takes place both in terms of an increase of religion law and through "incorporation" of religious law as part of the law of the land. On the other hand, Fox finds that "there has been little change in the basic structure of world government involvement in religion (GIR)—as measured by a state's official relationship with religion and the larger patterns of state treatment of religion".[126] To this we can add Fox's observation that few states endorse strict separation of state and religion.[127]

For the following fleeting look at the concrete results of Fox's study, it is worth underlining that he classifies states depending on the religious belonging of the majority population in the following way: Catholic, Orthodox, other Christian, Muslim, and other states. The last category covers states with other than Muslim or Christian religious traditions. Fox concedes that this naturally leaves unaccounted for important variations in the makeup of the religious landscape in different countries.[128]

Putting focus on the matter of majority religions, Fox asserts that countries with a Muslim majority show a consistently high level of official support, with Orthodox countries coming in second and Catholic countries third.[129] In 2002, for example, 57,4% states with a Muslim majority had one official religion, while the number for Orthodox and Catholic countries were 16,7% and 16,3% respectively.[130] However, other factors impact too, as Fox points out, alluding to the differences that can be found within and between regions when it comes to Muslim states and how their governments involve themselves with religion (GIR).

> This diversity exists both within and between world regions and the world's major religious traditions. For instance, the relationship between the state and Islam differs considerably between regions. The patterns of GIR in Muslim majority states in the Middle East, for example, are very different from those in the former Soviet bloc. They are also different

125 Fox 2008, 70–72.

126 Fox 2008, 313.

127 Fox 2008, 313.

128 Fox 2008, 64–65. The category "other Christian" also include countries where no Christian tradition has a majority as well as states where the denominational make-up is unclear. Fox 2008, 64.

129 Fox 2008, 67.

130 Fox 2008, 79.

> from state to state within these regions, even when looking only at Muslim states.[131]

In regards to the region of the Middle East and North Africa (MENA), Fox observes that all but three of the 20 governments he covers in his survey have an official religion; Islam or as in the case of Israel: Judaism.[132] With respect to constitutional guarantees of freedom of religion or belief, in turn, Fox notes that "while many Middle Eastern constitutions guarantee freedom of religion or belief, they usually include qualifiers, such as 'in accordance with local traditions and beliefs,' or 'subject to public policy and morals.' These qualifiers often mean that people have freedom of belief as long as it does not contradict Islam and Sharia law as applied in the state in question."[133] This leads Fox to conclude that: "The majority of the constitutions of the MENA promise religious freedom but state that this freedom is subordinate to Islam, local customs, public order, or some similar qualification, which effectively allows significant restrictions on religious freedom."[134]

In Sub-Saharan African countries, in turn, a "clear majority" of the 46 governments Fox surveys "do not substantially support religion based on the official separation measure". Moreover, of these 46 governments, 20 give no preference to religion whatsoever, as Fox puts it.[135] Five countries have Islam as the official religion, while in the last case, Zambia, the official religion is Christianity.[136]

In much of Latin Europe and Latin America, constitutions tend to provide special provisions for the Catholic Church, establishing the foundation for financial support, access to educational institutions or other tailor-made provisions. As Fox points out in his survey of Latin American countries, Catholicism is the official religion in only four states, the only states to have in effect an official religion,[137] and states across the continent have included clauses on non-discrimination and freedom of conscience and religion in their constitutions that afford certain rights and privileges to religious and other belief groups and individuals. Yet, beyond this, Fox detects a clear difference when it comes to the relationship between religion and state between the Catholic and

131 Fox 2008, 104.
132 Fox 2008, 218.
133 Fox 2008, 226.
134 Fox 2008, 248.
135 Fox 2008, 249.
136 Fox 2008, 250–51.
137 Fox 2008, 290.

non-Catholic countries:[138] "[N]early all Catholic states give preferential treatment to the Catholic church"[139] and concordats between the states and the Catholic Church play a role in setting the scene here.[140] In non-Catholic states, the government involvement with religion is lower.[141]

Restrictions on freedom of religion or belief may be broad or narrow in scope, neutrally formulated or indeed allude to the majority religion, as in the case of the constitution of Panama, where Article 34 in Fox's translation "guarantees religious freedom, as long as people respect 'Christian morality and public order.'"[142] Or Cuba where "Article 35 [of the 1992 Constitution] declares SRAS [separation of religion and state] and protects the freedom of religion and worship 'without other limitation than respect for Christian morality and public order.'"[143] Constitutions may also reflect the traditional make-up of societies by recognizing indigenous religion, as in the case of Paraguay where "Article 63 protects the rights of 'Indian peoples,' including their religious rights."[144]

Moving on to North America, in the US, whose foundational constitutional arrangement was partly elaborated in explicit contrast to Europe, the establishment clause is meant to counteract favouritism of a particular religion,[145] be it of Islam or Catholicism. For this reason, there is also a difference detectable within the group of what Fox denotes "Western democracies". He notes that more than "two-thirds of these governments can be placed into one of two clusters: six governments with active state religions and 13 governments who give preferential treatment to one or more religions."[146] In turn, "of the 18 states with no official religion, 14 of them have references to religion in their constitutions beyond the standard protections of religious freedom and against discrimination against religious minorities and a fifteenth, New Zealand, has no clause separating religion and state."[147]

---

138 Fox 2008, 296, 311.

139 Fox 2008, 290.

140 See e.g. Fox 2008, 304–305.

141 Fox 2008, 296, 311.

142 Fox 2008, 303–304.

143 Fox 2008, 310.

144 Fox 2008, 304.

145 Cross 2015, 54. Adopting Fox's terminology from his 2011 article on 'Separation of Religion and State and Secularism in Theory and Practice', what we encounter here is an example so called "absolute SRAS" a model which "requires that the state neither support nor hinder any religion". Fox 2011, 385.

146 Fox 2008, 136.

147 Fox 2008, 137.

With regard to countries in the "Former Soviet Bloc", Fox concludes that for 1990–2002, most of the constitutions of these countries included clauses "declaring SRAS [separation of religion and state], religious freedom, and equality of all religions before the law. These types of clauses exist respectively in 20, 25, and 24 of these countries' constitutions and all of the former Soviet Bloc countries have at least two of these clauses. Many countries that lack one of these clauses in their constitutions have enacted them as laws."[148]

In both of the last two groups of countries, we encounter states which Fox classifies as Orthodox. With regard to these and the patterns of religion-state relations that can be found there, Fox observes that:

> First, many states wish to protect their indigenous culture from outside influences. This pattern is particularly prominent in the Orthodox Christian states of Eastern Europe. The indigenous religious cultures of these states were eroded by the policies of past communist governments, but since the early 1990s most of these states are following policies of reestablishing indigenous cultures. They tend to support Orthodox Christianity and have policies that vary from tolerance to support of other religions with a historical presence in the state, but they often severely restrict religions considered new to the state.[149]

Finally, in Asia, nine of the governments surveyed by Fox had an official religion.[150] In Cambodia, for example, the constitution in

> Article 43 declares Buddhism the state religion but guarantees religious freedom provided that it 'does not affect other religious beliefs or violate public order and security.' Article 68 states that 'the State shall disseminate and develop the Pali schools and the Buddhist Institutes.' There are several symbolic mentions of religion in the constitution.[151]

Moreover, Article 31 guarantees religious equality.[152] As regards Hinduism, Fox's study includes two Asian states where Hinduism is "supported" but does not hold the status of official religion: India and Nepal. Fox's overview of these two constitutions reveal guarantees against religious discrimination and

148 Fox 2008, 180.

149 Fox 2008, 353.

150 Fox 2008, 181.

151 Fox 2008, 205.

152 Fox 2008, 205.

articles that provide for religious freedom (accompanied with certain limiting clauses), but also articles which display the support for and position of Hinduism in the countries in question.[153] Summing up his survey of constitutional arrangements and constitutional guarantees pertaining to religion in Asian states for the years 1990–2002, Fox concludes that:

> Asian states with different religious identities behave differently toward religion. Muslim states tend to be the most strongly supportive of state religions and, on average, place the most restrictions on religious minorities. With the exception of those states that are communist or have military governments, Buddhist states tend to support Buddhism but less intensely than Muslim states support Islam. Hindu states support Hinduism but do not declare it to be an official religion. Christian states tend to support Christianity or religion in general and tend to be tolerant of minorities. Communist and authoritarian states tend to try to control and restrict religion. The states with the most SRAS tend to be those that do not fit into any of the above categories and have a less distinct religious identity.[154]

In conclusion, Fox's survey shows that: "Of the 148 states for which there is sufficient information on the content of their constitutions, 133 promise some form of freedom of worship, 92 promise no discrimination on the basis of religion or equality for all religions, and 52 declare the state secular or prohibit the establishment of a religion."[155] The authority of the state over religion is limited and vice versa, and the governance of religion is regulated in various ways at the level of constitutions.

Constitutive Juridification of "Religious Law"

Now, in tandem with constitutive juridifications of religion through "religion law", a considerable number of constitutions feature provisions on the recognition of specific religious bodies of law. In particular, a majority of Muslim majority states secure an important role for the Islamic *Shari'a* as either "a" or "the" foundation of law, acting as a check on the adoption and adjudication of all civil law,[156] a role that has been the subject of considerable debate following the so-called Arab spring.

153 Fox 2008, 208–209.
154 Fox 2008, 216.
155 Fox 2008, 360.
156 For an overview, see e.g. Temperman 2010, 49–55.

This is pointed out by several scholars. In his survey of the years 1992–2002, Fox does not specifically differentiate between an increase in constitutive juridification of religious law and juridification of religious law at other levels of law (juridification B). What he does observe, is that the greatest increase in what he titles religious legislation took place in Muslim states even though the extent of such increase differed from country to country depending on, among other things, the extent to which religious legislation already was a more or less fixed feature of that state, like in the case of the MENA region.[157]

Moreover, even if the constitution does not single out any religion as the official religion of the state, juridification of religious law may take place at the sub-constitutional level:

> Even when national governments respect their constitutions, local governments often do not. For example, Nigeria's 1999 constitution bans both the national and local governments from adopting 'any religion as [the] state religion', but from 2000 many of Nigeria's Muslim-majority states began adopting aspects of sharia (Muslim religious) law as state law.[158]

Cross, in turn, notes that religious laws are seldom incorporated into national law in African countries, with the exception of nations influenced strongly by Islam.[159] Adding a further regional perspective, Fox asserts that "[r]eligious legislation is not uncommon in Latin America, but it is relatively homogeneous. The majority of all religious laws in Latin America fall into 1 of 5 categories that account for 105 of the 119 religious laws coded for the region by the RAS project."[160] Additionally and on a more general level, Cross observes with reference to Fox (2011) that:

> the presence of constitutional prohibitions did not eliminate religious legislation. He [Fox] did find a significant effect for some constitutional provisions. States with an official constitutional religion plainly had more legislation restricting religion. However, a formal declaration of separation of church and state had little effect, compared with constitutions that had no such reference.[161]

157 Fox 2008, 326.

158 Fox 2011, 395, citing Fox 2008, 272–73.

159 Cross 2015, 49.

160 Fox 2008, 290.

161 Cross 2015, 150; Fox 2011.

Fox finds that while autocratic states show higher levels of religious legislation, "democracies are nearly as likely to legislate religious laws as nondemocracies".[162] Indeed, the only state to lack any religious legislation, as Fox defines this for purposes of his survey, is the United States (US).[163]

Some will find that incorporating the religious law of a particular religion into the constitution will result in unequal treatment of religious minorities.[164] It may restrict, for example, the right to convert.[165] However, it should not be forgotten that discrimination of religious and belief minority positions occurs across the spectrum from countries akin to a theocracy to countries with an official atheist ideology.[166] Moreover, the subsequent entanglement of governments with the religion or religions which are favoured at a constitutional level may in effect set limits to religious self-governance, something which is not necessarily considered a positive thing from the perspective of those "favoured" faiths either.

Still, in his survey of constitutional bills of rights, Cross expresses uncertainty as to their actual effects and hence their value. He finds the scarce evidence available at this point inconclusive and identifies a need for more wide-scale empirical research.[167] One way to look into this could be to pursue a study of interlinked processes of juridification. Already in the survey literature, we encounter observations as to how juridification A, depending on the concrete shape, seems to affect other dimensions of juridification. According to Cross, the material that he surveys indicate a connection between juridification of religion (A) and de-juridification of religion (B) to the effect that "[e]stablishment clauses were consistently associated with less religious legislation".[168] Hence, disestablishment at the constitutional level comes accompanied by "dejuridification of religious law" in dimensions A and B. Constitutive de-juridifications of religion in religion law is associated with constitutive de-juridifications of

162 Fox 2008, 347; "The major difference between democracies and nondemocracies in this respect is not a question of willingness to legislate on religious matters but a question of how much religious legislation they will place on the books. Thus, the average democracy legislates several types of religious laws, but the mean level of *religious legislation* is higher among nondemocracies than it is among democracies."

163 Fox 2008, 346.

164 Cross 2015, 35.

165 See e.g. Cross 2015, 38.

166 For an overview, see e.g. Cross 2015, 35–47.

167 Cross 2015, 151–52.

168 Cross 2015, 178.

religious law and de-juridification of religious law as regards juridification in the sense of an expansion and differentiation of law (B).

Fox identifies a similar connection between constitutive juridification of religion A and juridification of religion B, when observing that "states with official religions are more likely to have religious legislation", by which he understands what we in this article denote as juridification of religious law.[169] In a similar vein, Temperman points out that the kind of constitutional acknowledgment where religious law becomes the yardstick for state law, forms "one of the most far-reaching measures of ensuring a positive identification with a single religion" and will have profound effects on all branches of government including the judiciary.[170] However, even a constitution that is relatively silent on religious matters may "sanction the application of religious laws by state courts", like in the case of Sierra Leone.[171]

Of course, what religion or religions are more specifically affected and in which potentially disparate ways is a matter for contextual empirical investigation. As Fox notes with regard to his own RAS data: it measures governmental behaviour in the area of regulation or deregulation of religion at, for example, the level of constitutions, but does not accurately tell about the motivations for such action however important they may be (although regulative restrictions targeting minority practices may be a case to the contrary at least in some respects).[172]

In turn, Ran Hirschl, who has carried out a comparative study of how constitutional protections of religion are applied, has concluded that: "constitutional law and courts in virtually all such polities have become bastions of relative secularism, pragmatism, and moderation, thereby emerging as effective shields against the spread of religiosity and increased popular support for principles of theocratic governance."[173] According to Cross and others, constitutional juridification of religion transfers powers to courts to adjudicate on matters of religion in a way that they would perhaps not have otherwise, and this opens up for protection also of unbelief given that clauses on freedom of religion often enough are interpreted as protecting both the right to believe and the right not to believe.[174] Drawing on Hirschl, Cross calls this transfer a

169 Fox 2008, 55.

170 Temperman 2010, 49–50.

171 Temperman 2010, 109.

172 Fox 2008, 60–61.

173 Ran Hirschl, *Constitutional Theocracy* (Harvard University Press 2010) 13.

174 Cross 2015, 30–31.

"'judicialization' of politics",[175] or in the categories of Blichner and Molander juridification A → juridification D.

Issues for Further Research

Based on this overview of constitutive juridification and the way associated issues have been taken up in current literature, we would encourage law and religion scholars to broaden further their perspective as regards constitutive juridification beyond the current strong focus on specific constitutionally enshrined principles of non-discrimination and religious rights and their interpretation, as well as formal divisions of power and competence.

It is our contention that the concurrent study of different dimensions of juridification as proposed by Blichner and Molander can deepen our understanding by adding further layers and voices to the analysis and help us tease out further nuances as regards state-religion relations, divisions of authority and how constitutional recognition or nonrecognition of religion affect juridification or de-juridification of religion in the other dimensions and vice versa, including how constitutionalisation of religious law result in *de facto* shifts of authority between different branches of government and societal actors. While few states may consider themselves officially laic, for instance, a closer study might show that many constitutional amendments also in other states than those with a constitutionally enshrined principle of secularism aim at easing the ties between state and religion and in effect in this respect strive for de-juridification.

Hence, we suggest that it would be worthwhile inquiring in a more comprehensive fashion into the concrete broader effects of constitutional juridification of religion.[176] For it seems safe to say that while some form of relationship between constitutional change, the differentiation of legal subfields and increased judicial power can safely be assumed in theory, their interrelationship is likely to be volatile and subject to considerable fluctuation at the empirical level. Likewise any study of "constitutional religion" would benefit from inquiries into how this is effected by other processes of juridification of religion, including the expansion and differentiation of regulatory measures targeting

---

175 Cross 2015, 121; Hirschl 2006.

176 One such study is Benjamin Schonthal, *Buddhism, Politics and the Limits of the Law: The Pyrrhic Constitutionalism of Sri Lanka* (Cambridge University Press 2016).

"religion" across a range of domestic subfields of law (see 3B), alternative visions of *theo-legality* and resort to *lawfare* (see 3C).[177]

3B *The Expansion and Differentiation of Law*

According to the model of juridification suggested by Blichner and Molander, the concomitant expansion and differentiation of law will tend to represent the first, initial step of the process, with increased conflict solving by recourse to law, increased judicial autonomy and constitutional regulations on religion as subsequent steps in the process (see section 2), which in aggregate leads to the increased "legal framing" of religion (see 3E).

The expansion and differentiation of law represent two distinct, yet interrelated modes of juridification. The *expansion* of law (B1) denotes the increasing reach of legal rules, corresponding closely to the "classical" model of juridification developed by Habermas (see above). As the scope of legal regulation expands, it becomes applied to increasingly new areas, ranging from family law to laws governing employment and the environment.[178] This expansion may be the result of fresh legislation introduced at the parliamentary level, or a consequence of the implementation of rules derived from international treaties. In either case, the expansion of law subordinates previously unregulated activities to legal rule.

As the scope of legal regulation expands, however, it also tends to become more *differentiated*, as new subdivisions of pre-existing legal regulations (B2) are developed in order to respond to an increasing number of cases within each legal area. Hence, while initial regulations introduced in order to protect the rights of marginalized subgroups in society did not distinguish sharply between different kinds of minorities, the last decades has seen increasing attention to the rights of indigenous peoples, whose specific challenges have been addressed in instruments like the United Nations (UN) Declaration on the Rights of Indigenous Peoples (2007, see below).

Regulating Religion

The legislative interest in religion as a regulatory object, while a regular feature of modern nation states, has been propelled to the forefront of political debate since the end of the Cold War and the gradual demographic changes in Western Europe. Whereas legislators at the international, regional and

177 Terminology borrowed from John L. Comaroff, 'Reflections on the Rise of Legal Theology: Law and Religion in the Twenty-First Century' (2009) 53 *Social Analysis* 193.

178 Blichner and Molander 2008, 43.

domestic level spent more time discussing racism and culture in the 1960s and up to the 1980s, the 1990s and 2000s saw a sharp rise in the number of contentious political debates and attendant legislative changes related to religion. These changes have both expanded and differentiated the legal framework on religion, as states have relied in unequal measures on the adoption of new legislation that subordinates previously unregulated spheres to legal regulation and on the differentiation of pre-existing legal rules to respond to the increasing number of cases. Over the course of the last decade, laws have been adopted to curb the harmful influence of religious sects,[179] to regulate the display of religious symbols in the public square,[180] male circumcision,[181] ritual slaughter,[182] the registration of religious communities,[183] the relation between labour and equality legislation and the freedom of religion or belief,[184] the negotiation of family relationships in law as well as between different regulatory systems,[185] and a broad variety of additional issues.[186]

Whether these new regulations of religion represent the expansion (B1) or differentiation (B2) of law, however, depends on the country in question, and the particular framing of legislative change. Regulations on the display of ritual slaughter, for instance, date back centuries in some parts of Europe, while being fairly recent in others,[187] constituting differentiation of pre-existing

179 Willy Fautré, 'Belgium's Anti-Sect War' (1999) 12 *Social Justice Research* 377.

180 Alessandro Ferrari and Sabrina Pastorelli (eds), *The Burqa Affair across Europe: Between Public and Private Space* (Ashgate 2013).

181 Stephen Munzer, 'Secularization, Anti-Minority Sentiment, and Cultural Norms in the German Circumcision Controversy' (2015) 37 *University of Pennsylvania Journal of International Law* 503.

182 Norman Doe, 'Towards a "Common Law" on Religion in the European Union' (2009) 37 *Religion, State and Society* 147.

183 Julian Rivers, *The Law of Organized Religions: Between Establishment and Secularism* (Oxford University Press 2010).

184 Katayoun Alidadi and Marie-Claire Foblets, 'Framing Multicultural Challenges in Freedom of Religion Terms. Limitations of Minimal Human Rights for Managing Religious Diversity in Europe' (2012) 30 *Netherlands Quarterly of Human Rights* 460.

185 Rossella Bottoni, Rinaldo Cristofori and Silvio Ferrari (eds), *Religious Rules, State Law, and Normative Pluralism—A Comparative Overview* (Springer 2016).

186 Silvio Ferrari (ed), *Routledge Handbook of Law and Religion* (Routledge 2015); Heiner Bielefeldt, Nazila Ghanea and Michael Wiener, *Freedom of Religion or Belief: An International Law Commentary* (Oxford University Press 2015).

187 Laura Kurth and Pieter Glasbergen, 'Dealing with Tensions of Multiculturalism: The Politics of Ritual Slaughter in the Netherlands' (2015) *European Journal of Cultural Studies* 1; David Smith, '"Cruelty of the Worst Kind": Religious Slaughter, Xenophobia, and the German Greens' (2007) 40 *Central European History* 89.

legislation in some jurisdictions, and expansion of the scope of law in others. Additionally, the extent to which legislative change represents expansion or differentiation can be framed differently in public and legislative debate, as attested to by heated discussions on male circumcision, whose prohibition is framed as an illegitimate expansion of law's remit into the private sphere by some participants in the debate,[188] but as a differentiation of the human right to health to also encompass this particular procedure by other participants.[189] As such, the expansion and differentiation of laws on religion cannot be substantiated in general terms, but must be subject to specific, empirical identification in each separate instance.

Parallel to the expansion and differentiation of laws on "religion", rules and regulations outlining the proper boundaries of "religious law" have also increased, as states have taken a keen interest in the nature and scope of legal rules developed within the boundaries of religious communities. While religio-legal rules have long been recognized in African and Asian states, where the legal rules of religious communities have long constituted regular features of family law,[190] the recent turn towards the recognition of religious legal rules in Western states like Canada and the United Kingdom (UK) represents a new and different view of the role of religious laws in liberal democracies.[191] As with the generation of legal rules on religion, however, the regulation of religious laws will take place as expansions of legal regulations in some states, and the differentiation of previously existing legislation in others.

While these structural challenges invalidate simplified conceptions of the juridification of religion as *either* the expansion *or* the differentiation of law, we suggest that the juridification of religion through the combined effects of the expansion *and* differentiation of laws on religion is well underway as a general phenomenon that can be observed globally. We argue that this phenomenon has gathered momentum over the course of the last decades, not least due to the increasing role of international human rights law, which has both been expanded in terms of material provisions that explicitly regulate religion,

188 Allan J. Jacobs and Kavita S. Arora, 'Ritual Male Infant Circumcision and Human Rights' (2015) 15 *The American Journal of Bioethics* 30.

189 J. Steven Svoboda, 'Growing World Consensus to Leave Circumcision Decision to the Affected Individual' (2015) 15 *The American Journal of Bioethics* 46.

190 Iza R. Hussin, *The Politics of Islamic Law: Local Elites, Colonial Authority and the Making of the Muslim State* (University of Chicago Press 2016); Michael G. Peletz, *Islamic Modern: Religious Courts and Cultural Politics in Malaysia* (Princeton University Press 2002).

191 Marie Ashe M. and Anisa Hélie, 'Realities of Religio-Legalism: Religious Courts and Women's Rights in Canada, the United Kingdom, and the United States' (2014) 20 *U.Cal.-Davis J. International Law & Policy* 139.

providing legislators with the vocabulary and taxonomy to develop new legislation on religion through the expansion of the existing legal framework, while also differentiating the reach of pre-existing provisions. In the following, we provide a brief overview of the main tendencies in the combined expansion and differentiation of legal regulations of religion, with a particular emphasis on how these processes interact with the other dimensions of juridification identified by Blichner and Molander.

The Expansion and Differentiation of Laws on Religion

There is no available metric for the concrete measurement of whether legal rules on religion have expanded and/or differentiated over the course of the last decades.[192] Nevertheless, the combined effects of (1) the general growth of legal regulation and (2) the growing influence of international and transnational legal regulations suggest that the volume of legal regulations on religion is also growing steadily. This growth is not only the result of legislators seeking to regulate new areas of social life through the adoption of new laws or the differentiation of pre-existing laws, but can also be attributed to the accelerating rate of change in religious demography and the concomitantly growing influence of religious communities and organizations as significant subgroups in society whose interface with the legal system is growing, despite the sharp increase in individually determined forms of religiosity untethered from formal authority structures (see 3E).

(1) *The Growth of Legal Regulation*

The general growth of legal regulation in contemporary society is widespread and undisputed. Governments and parliaments increasingly outsource hot-button political issues to the legal system, passing policies and legislation that trigger the development of additional numbers of legal and semi-legal regulations in subordinate, administrative entities. Additionally, the growing role of scientific research into everything from the environment and urban

192 While the US Pew Forum on Religion and Public Life have issued annual reports on "restrictions of religion" since 2009, these reports are based on a conception of religion as "explanations of existence based on supernatural assumptions that include statements about the nature and workings of the supernatural and about ultimate meaning", a notion that is far removed from dominant legal concepts of religion, whether in domestic or international law, rendering the metric inapplicable for legal analysis. See Pew Forum: *Global Restrictions on Religion: Methodology*, http://www.pewforum.org/2009/12/17/methodology/, accessed 13 June 2017 and Brian J. Grim and Roger Finke, 'International Religion Indexes: Government Regulation, Government Favoritism, and Social Regulation of Religion' (2006) 2 *Interdisciplinary Journal of Research on Religion* 1, 6.

planning to healthcare and social services has buttressed the role of law as the "handmaiden of scientific regulation".[193] Through this general growth, the interface between law and religion has grown exponentially, propelling the study of law and religion to a "crescendo in a rich and evocative symphony",[194] the scope and scale of which has moved beyond easy classification or counting. Indeed, the growing interaction between legal rules and religion has sparked the creation of a number of dedicated research centers, journals, conferences and associations. Within the field of law and religion, however, the general growth of legal regulation has not been a major concern, as scholars have pointed to the "comeback" or "resurgence" of religion in the public sphere as the main factor causing the increased interest in the interrelationship between law and religion (see below).[195]

We suggest that the theory that increases in legal regulations of religion have been developed as responses to the perceived comeback or return of religion to the public sphere, while important, has led to insufficient attention to the ways in which the legal regulation of religion correlates with the larger growth in legal regulations across different subfields of law. Arguably, exploring these correlations opens up a set of fresh perspectives on the interrelationship between law and religion that have so far been undertheorized in the field, from the fundamental indeterminacy of legal regulation to the influence of migratory legal concepts, or "irritants" that move across systemic boundaries, and to the process of "bureaucratization", whereby the increase in legal regulation transfers decision-making authority to specialized administrative entities that operate according to their own, internal rules. We will deal with these perspectives in turn.

First, the question of *indeterminacy* is foundational to legal theory: The outcome of legal regulation, however minute and specific, will always be indeterminate because no statute can pretend to cover all imaginable instances of its application.[196] Applied to the growth of legal regulation, the expected outcome would be that growing legal regulation leads to growing indeterminacy, the endpoint of which would be "juristocracy", whereby the judiciary gradually

193 Boaventura de Sousa Santos, *Toward a New Legal Common Sense: Law, Globalization, And Emancipation* (Butterworth 2002).

194 Marie A. Failinger, 'Twenty-Five Years of Law and Religion Scholarship: Some Reflections' (2014) 30 *Touro Law Review* 9.

195 Fallinger 2014; James T. Richardson, 'Managing Religion and the Judicialization of Religious Freedom' (2015) 54 *Journal for the Scientific Study of Religion* 1.

196 Mark Modak-Truran, 'Secularization, Legal Indeterminacy, and Habermas' Discourse Theory of Law' (2007) 35 *Florida State University Law Review* 73.

takes over control from elected politicians (see 3D).[197] Correspondingly, as the number of legal rules that regulate religion increase, the role of the judiciary in determining the role of religion increases, to the point where any perceived secularization of the legal system can be called into question because of the potential influence of the religious outlooks of the judiciary, as pointed out by Mark Modak-Truran.[198] Additionally, given the contestation and confusion regarding the nature and scope of "religion" for scholarly, legal and political purposes, the regulation of religion under different models of "secularism" risks leading to particularly unpredictable results, as an indeterminate system of regulation seeks to handle an indeterminate regulatory object.[199]

Importantly, however, while the rules and regulations laid down in the legal system will tend towards indeterminacy, the deployment of specific regulations that spell out the conditions of their application will arguably shift towards *underdeterminacy*, solidifying some regulatory aspects while leaving others open to interpretation. As Jason A. Springs has pointed out, the norm regulating limitations of the freedom of religion or belief in the ECHR article 9(2) is not indeterminate in the sense that any imaginable limitation may be applied, but rather underdetermined in that it provides for a wide range of contextually determined aspects to influence what may constitute legitimate limitations to the right.[200]

While Springs' account of how the French state has appropriated norms from the European level demonstrates the importance of contextual constraints on the determination of the nature and scope of norms, the large and growing attention towards "legal transplants" in socio-legal studies has served to highlight the profoundly transformative effects of migrating legal concepts, as the architecture of norms developed at the international level become effectively altered upon their travels to domestic law (see more below).[201] From this perspective, the radical transformation of norms upon their transplantation will undermine the stability of regulations that spell out the conditions of their application, thus rendering their application indeterminate and uncertain.

---

197 The term "juristocracy" was coined by Ran Hirschl in the article '"Juristocracy"—Political, Not Juridical' (2004) 13 *The Good Society* 6.

198 Modak-Truran 2007, 91.

199 Hussein A. Agrama, 'Secularism, Sovereignty, Indeterminacy: Is Egypt a Secular or a Religious State?' (2010) 52 *Comparative Studies in Society and History* 495.

200 Jason A. Springs, 'Tentacles of the Leviathan? Nationalism, Islamophobia, and the Insufficiency-yet-Indispensability of Human Rights for Religious Freedom in Contemporary Europe' (2016) 84 *Journal of the American Academy of Religion* 903.

201 David Nelken and Johannes Feest (eds), *Adapting Legal Cultures* (Hart 2001).

While a constant feature in the growth of legal regulation, the ways in which indeterminacy affects the legal regulation of religion play out differently across and within different jurisdictions, whose legal cultures and legal systems will provide different alternatives for the management of indeterminacy, crucially affecting their approaches to the regulation of religion. Mapping the ways in which different jurisdictions have handled the issue of indeterminacy in their regulatory activities towards religion, the literature on law and religion has paid significant attention to the discussion of whether "religion" poses a set of particularly thorny definitional challenges to the legal system. This discussion has been particularly contentious in the US, where critics have challenged the notion that religion is "special",[202] suggested its replacement with alternate concepts like "equal liberty",[203] or simply dismissed the capacity of law to regulate religion as such.[204]

Second, and closely related to the question of indeterminacy, the growth in legal regulations has stimulated the increased expansion and differentiation of legal concepts across interconnected legal systems. As the migration of legal concepts lead to fundamental changes in both the concepts themselves and in the receiving systems, several scholars have suggested different terms to denote this process, ranging from transposition, tuning and fitting[205] to transfers, transplants or translations,[206] to better emphasize the transformative nature of travelling legal concepts. Günther Teubner has stressed that such attempted transplants cannot be reduced either to a "mechanic" shift resembling the refitting of a machine part, nor to an "organic" move whose chances of fitting into the complexity of the receiving legal culture would be well-nigh impossible due to pre-existing procedures and interpretative traditions.

Writing about the import of contractual "good faith", which has a long and complicated pre-history in continental legal traditions, into the UK legal system where it was previously not in use, Teubner has dismissed a simplified

202 Micah Schwartzman, 'What if Religion isn't Special?' (2012) 79 *The University of Chicago Law Review* 1351.

203 Christopher L. Eisgruber and Larry G. Sager, *Religious Freedom and the Constitution* (Harvard University Press 2010).

204 Sullivan 2005.

205 Esin Örücü, 'Law as Transposition' (2002) 51 *International and Comparative Law Quarterly* 205.

206 Lena Foljanty, 'Legal Transfers as Processes of Cultural Translation: On the Consequences of a Metaphor' *Max Planck Institute for European Legal History Research Paper Series* No. 2015–09 (2015).

either/or model, settling for the more intermediate notion of "legal irritant",[207] in order to better capture the fuzzy effects of such imports in the receiving legal system. Travelling legal concepts become irritants not only because they cause tensions with the idiosyncrasies of the receiving legal system, but also because they become enmeshed with the increasingly complicated interface between law and society,[208] ranging from more or less firmly established ties with scientific and technological sectors of society, to healthcare, social issues and cultural questions. Arguably, the notion of irritant is not exclusive to conceptual migrations across large-scale systemic boundaries like different domestic legal orders, but may also be detected within the different substrata of established legal orders. Indeed, as the scope of legal regulation grows in scale, substance and complexity, so does its interface with surrounding society, generating potential overlaps between the layers of regulation offered by different sections of the same legal system.

Applied to the regulation of religion, the notion of "legal irritants" invites additional perspectives on the interface between law, religion and society that have so far not been explored within the field of law and religion. While Norman Doe has delivered important contributions to the development of a sociologically informed approach to law and religion,[209] scholars have yet to examine how the travels of legal regulations on religion across and within different legal systems have opened up new interactions, both internally within legal systems, across legal systems and between law and other social spheres. Unlike earlier regulations, which could capture the broad mainstream of religion through legislation by targeting formal organizations and individual practices related to major, clearly identifiable traditions of interpretation, the "religion" that is subject to legal regulation in modern society is distributed across a much broader variety of different spheres in society.

In order to satisfy their requirements under the International Covenant on Civil and Political Rights (1966), for instance, states are obliged to regularly report on:

- The existence of different religions within the State party's jurisdiction.
- The publication and circulation of religious material.

---

207 Günther Teubner, 'Legal Irritants: Good Faith in British Law or How Unifying Law Ends Up in New Divergencies' (1998) 61 *Modern Law Review* 11.

208 Teubner 1998, 21.

209 Russell Sandberg, *Religion, Law and Society* (Cambridge University Press 2014); Norman Doe, 'A Sociology of Law and Religion - Towards a New Discipline: Legal Responses to Religious Pluralism in Europe' (2004) 69 *Law & Justice* 68.

- The measures taken to prevent and to punish offences against the free exercise of one's religion.
- In cases where a State religion exists, how a person's freedom to practice another religion, to convert to another religion, or not to have a religion is guaranteed and on how the application of the principle of non-discrimination on religious grounds is ensured.
- Any procedures that must be followed for the legal recognition and authorization of various religious denominations in the country and their practical application, including information on any refusal of recognition that might have occurred during the reporting period.
- The main status differences between the dominant religion and other denominations, in particular with regard to the granting of subsidies and the protection of, and access to, places of worship, in particular for those belonging to religious minorities.
- The legal regulation and the practice of religious education, in particular where religion is taught in State schools, the possibility for children not to attend religious classes and how the right of parents to ensure the religious education of their children in conformity with their own convictions is guaranteed.
- The fiscal provisions applicable to religions.

...

- The status and legal position of conscientious objectors.
- The number of persons that applied for the status of, and those that were actually recognized as, conscientious objectors.
- The reasons considered to justify conscientious objection and the rights and duties of conscientious objectors as compared to those of persons who serve in the regular military service.[210]

These reporting requirements require states to identify "religion" across a variety of different social spheres, developing datasets, gathering statistical and qualitative information on policies and regulations on religion that go well beyond the confines of organized religions and individual religious practice, causing widespread "irritations" for state entities set to these monitoring tasks, which in turn buttresses the power of bureaucracies (see below).

210 United Nations Human Rights Committee. *Guidelines for the treaty-specific document to be submitted by States parties under article 40 of the International Covenant on Civil and Political Rights* (CCPR/C/2009/1, 22 November 2010), para. 83–84.

Although the literature on legal irritants is strongly oriented towards the domestic effects of regulations developed at the international level,[211] similar "irritations" may also be detected across different sections of domestic law: As "religion" becomes subject to legal regulations within highly specialized legal discourses, the means and modes of its identification and determination become gradually more complex, and their overlaps and internal cohesion more uncertain. Russell Sandberg has asked whether this development may indicate the formation of a "single, coherent subdiscipline" comparable to that of other thematic fields of law like sports law or family law, arguing that growing homogeneity across different definitions of religion across separate legal branches may indicate that a "new body of law" is being formed.[212] This proposition is informed by an examination of legal cases determining the scope of the "two pillars of religion law", i.e. religious freedom and religious discrimination law, neither of which exhaust the widespread and profound expansion and differentiation of regulatory measures targeting "religion".

Indeed, the specific effects of the increased regulation of religion within new legal fields is still under researched, ranging from the ways in which anti-terror legislation and restrictions on the gathering of personal data and to the determination of zoning requirements for religious buildings and the determination of religion-based asylum claims, neither of which necessarily involve references and analogies to erstwhile "religion law". Throughout these fields, the identification of "religion" takes on roles that go far beyond the confines of mainstream religion law, as the external constraints of each subfield override the terms and conditions provided by religion law.

Third, and building on the combined effects of indeterminacy and the spread of religion as a legal irritant across and within different legal systems, increased legal regulations invariably leads to the *bureaucratization* of religion. Whilst popular conceptions of law and the legal system tend to revolve around the formal echelons of elected parliamentary assemblies and the official court system, the vast majority of legal decisions in late modern society are determined in the wider legal system, from tax offices and bureaux handling social security issues to out-of-court settlements of child custody and the arbitration of contract terms. Unlike parliamentary debates and court cases, these decisions are not made in the public view, and tend to be guided by "soft law", i.e. circulars and case notes that provide vital contextual input to decision-makers. As religion enters these discourses as a side-effect of its increased regulation,

211 See e.g. Jorge Precht Pizarro, 'Constitutional Reception of International Law Provisions on Religious Freedom' in Durham et al. (eds) 2013, 67–88.

212 Sandberg 2011, 10, 197.

its determination becomes subject to a range of predetermined procedures. The paradigmatic case of this bureaucratization of religion is colonial, ranging from the contributions of British civil servants to the solidification of religious identities in India in the 18th and 19th century[213] via the ambiguous post-colonial legacy of "Islamic law"[214] and to the instability of "religion" for regulatory purposes on the colonial frontier of southern Africa.[215]

With the general growth of legal regulations, the role of civil servants overseeing the implementation of administrative law has become vital to determining the legal scope of religion, placing the bureaucratization of religion at the heart and center of the juridification of religion. As Bruno Latour has observed, French administrative law is a "completely autonomous and separate system from the judiciary ... almost totally unknown by the French people themselves",[216] rendering the judgements of the Conseil d'Etat obscure and unpredictable. While the independence and separateness of administrative law varies considerably across different legal systems, the obscurity, level of technical specialization and isolation of certain branches of administrative law from that of the erstwhile legal system is a general feature of modern law.

The isolation and specialization of administrative law is particularly relevant to the regulation of religion in two ways. First, the level of specialization within administrative regulations and their adjudication provide different spaces for and approaches to religion as a regulatory object. Managing the influence of religion upon the work of airport security guards requires a different concept of religion than the provision of pastoral care in state institutions, from hospitals to prisons, where context-specific constraints create different environments for the handling of religion through law and administration. While the majority of cases within these fields are decided out of court, some of these issues eventually find their ways into the regular court system, causing considerable "irritation" and uncertainty as generalist lawyers and judges struggle with the intricacies of administrative procedure. One striking example of this process is the refugee status determination procedure, whereby the decisions of specialized, administrative refugee agencies can be brought before the courts, whose

213 Franklin A. Presler, *Religion under Bureaucracy: Policy and Administration for Hindu Temples in South India* (Cambridge University Press 1987); Philip C. Almond, *The British Discovery of Buddhism* (Cambridge University Press 1988); Peter J. Marshall, *The British Discovery of Hinduism in the Eighteenth Century* (Cambridge University Press 1970).

214 Hussin 2016.

215 David Chidester, *Savage Systems: Colonialism and Comparative Religion in Southern Africa* (University Press of Virginia 1996).

216 Bruno Latour, *The Making of Law: An Ethnography of the Conseil d'Etat* (Polity 2010) vii.

capacity to interpret the exceedingly complicated subject matter of refugee law and the interpretation of country of origin information is limited.[217]

Second, and following from the incapacity of the general legal system to engage fully with the intricacies of administrative law, courts tend to be deferential towards the decisions of administrative entities, particularly in cases where the regulatory question is considered to require specialized knowledge or training. As the specialization of administrative law increases steadily, so does the level of this "bureaucratic discretion", whereby civil servants take over the role as the principal adjudicators of law.[218] This discretion expands the reach of law not only in terms of what aspects of society become subject to regulation, but also in terms of who is capable of delivering authoritative interpretations of these regulations, effectively altering the distribution of power (see also 3D). In the bureaucratization of religion, this is particularly the case in the taxation of religious organizations, the determination of which is subject to the exceedingly intricate regulations of tax law, which tends to be far removed from the originally adopted legislation, as in the example of the hierarchy of regulations within the US Internal Revenues Service (IRS)

> First is the legislation itself, or the sections of the Internal Revenue Code. Then come the Regulations, which are issued under the authority of the Secretary of the Treasury, and which currently fill four large volumes. Next are Revenue Procedures, which may be promulgated by the Commissioner of Internal Revenue. Then come Revenue Rulings. Finally, there are Private Letter Rulings, or letters from the National Office of the IRS to a District Director of the Service stating an opinion as to how a tax matter should be resolved; with the deletion of the identification of the taxpayer or exempt organization, a private letter ruling may be "discovered" under the Freedom of Information Act but may not be cited as a precedent, unless the secretary otherwise establishes by regulation, IRC § 6110(j)(3) (West 1990), and is subject to change as the National Office sees fit.[219]

217 Robert Gibb and Anthony Good, 'Do the Facts Speak for Themselves? Country of Origin Information in French and British Refugee Status Determination Procedures' (2013) 25 *International Journal of Refugee Law* 291.

218 Sean Gailmard, 'Expertise, Subversion, and Bureaucratic Discretion' (2002) 18 *Journal of Law, Economics, and Organization* 536.

219 Edwards McGlynn Gaffney, 'Governmental Definition of Religion: The Rise and Fall of the IRS Regulations on an "Integrated Auxiliary of a Church"' (1991) 25 *Valparaiso University Law Review* 203, 204 (fn. 3).

To aid religious organizations with their paperwork, the IRS has published its own 40-page "Tax Guide", including a 14-point list of definitional criteria for the identification of a "church".[220] While the IRS criteria have been controversial and subject to intense litigation for decades, their review by the courts have been incomplete at the best of times, retaining considerable institutional autonomy to the IRS in developing and applying its regulations of religion.

(2) *International Legal Regulations*

In tandem with the rise of the modern welfare state, the development of legal regulations at the international level tends to be used as an indication of the increased scope of law in the literature on juridification. To Blichner and Molander, one of the primary examples of the international dimension of juridification is the growth of EU regulations and their insertion into domestic law.[221] While displaying similar tendencies towards indeterminacy, the development of legal irritants and bureaucratization as domestic law (see above), the nature and scope of international legal regulations of religion are additionally affected by their entanglements with geopolitical conditions, by the internal relationship between different regulations on religion, and by their monitoring by international enforcement mechanisms.

First, geopolitical conditions have been essential to the creation of legal norms of religion at the international level, the majority of which have come about as direct consequences of the brokerage of peace treaties following major armed conflicts, ranging from the Peace of Augsburg (1555), the Edict of Nantes (1598) and the Peace of Westphalia (1648) to the settlements following the First (1919) and Second (1945) World Wars.[222] Throughout these settlements, the purpose and objects of regulation have shifted repeatedly, leading

---

220 Internal Revenue Service. *501(c)(3) Tax Guide for Churches and Religious Organizations* (Rev. 8–2015), https://www.irs.gov/pub/irs-pdf/p1828.pdf, accessed 12 June 2017. The guide lists the following criteria for religious organizations: "distinct legal existence; recognized creed and form of worship; definite and distinct ecclesiastical government; formal code of doctrine and discipline; distinct religious history; membership not associated with any other church or denomination; organization of ordained ministers; ordained ministers selected after completing prescribed courses of study; literature of its own; established places of worship; regular congregations; regular religious services; Sunday schools for the religious instruction of the young; and schools for the preparation of its ministers."

221 Blichner and Molander 2008, 37.

222 Stephen C. Neff, 'An Evolving International Norm of Religious Freedom: Problems and Prospects' (1977) 7 *California Western International Law Journal* 543.

up to the post-war conception of human rights[223] that currently constitutes the main frame of reference for the international legal regulation of religion. Significantly, the "religion" regulated by international law up to the Second World War was decidedly collective, indicating the identity of certain subgroups in society and the rights they should be assigned in order to prevent social and political strife.[224]

Following the Second World War, during which this collective conception of rights protection had utterly failed to provide security to persecuted minorities, the ensuing adoption of the UDHR evaded the rights of minorities in its entirety, while introducing a new and radically individualist conception of freedom of religion or belief in Article 18, dovetailing a general ban on discrimination based on "race, colour, sex, language, religion, political or other opinion, national or social origin, property, birth or other status" in Article 2. The adoption and implementation of these norms against the background of societal upheavals have been decisive to the formation of "religion law" both at the international and at the domestic level, obliging states to generate and monitor legal guarantees for religious freedom and against religious discrimination.

Second, however, while the scope of these norms have been discussed for some time in the legal literature,[225] their internal relationship, including the nature of the object under regulation and their influence on the regulation of religion in other international instruments are not sufficiently known or understood. The determination of the "religion" regulated by international law has been dominated by an individualist and belief-centered conception of religious freedom at the expense of collective concepts of religion enshrined

---

223 The coherence, roots and political influence of human rights in the post-war era has recently come under increasing scrutiny. See in particular Samuel Moyn, *The Last Utopia: Human Rights in History* (The Belknap Press 2010).

224 Mark Mazower, 'The Strange Triumph of Human Rights, 1933–1950' (2004) 47 *The Historical Journal* 379.

225 Heiner Bielefeldt, Nazila Ghanea and Michael Wiener, *Freedom of Religion or Belief: An International Law Commentary* (Oxford University Press 2015); Anat Scolnicov, *The Right to Religious Freedom in International Law* (Routledge 2010); Paul M. Taylor, *Freedom of Religion—UN and European Human Rights Law and Practice* (Cambridge University Press 2005); Tore Lindholm, W. Cole Durham, Jr. and Bahiyyih G. Tahzib-Lie (eds), *Facilitating Freedom of Religion or Belief: A Deskbook* (Martinus Nijhoff 2004); Bahiyyih G. Tahzib, *Freedom of Religion or Belief: Ensuring Effective International Legal Protection* (Martinus Nijhoff 1996).

in the rights of religious minorities.[226] Indeed, when the former UN Special Rapporteur on the Freedom of Religion or Belief, Heiner Bielefeldt, submitted his annual report to the UN General Assembly in 2012, he attested to the prevalence of a belief-centered approach to religion when he rephrased the issue of religious minorities to "religious or belief minorities".[227]

Scholars have shown limited interest in how norms developed under the "religion or belief umbrella" identified by Nazila Ghanea[228] interact with other norms on religion at the international level. The relationship between different concepts of religion in international law has always been contentious, from the discussions regarding religion as both a source and object of rights during the drafting of the UDHR[229] via the protracted debates on the intersections between racial and religious discrimination in the 1960s and up to the present,[230] and to the still-ongoing efforts to create a standalone protective instrument on religion.[231]

As the number of international norms regulating religion has increased in the post-war era, the utility and precision of the belief-centered approach to religion has become more uncertain. In particular, this approach has recently come under pressure during the refugee crisis, as refugee status determination procedures have increasingly been forced to deal with the correlation between religious freedom and the prohibition of religious discrimination and the duty to provide protection for people who are "persecuted for reasons of race, religion, nationality, membership of a particular social group or political opinion" under the Refugee Convention (1951). While the correlation between the standards of the UDHR and ensuing instruments on religious freedom and the notion of "religion" in the Refugee Convention is clearly established at the level of norms, its practical application is highly volatile and

---

226 Nazila Ghanea, 'Are Religious Minorities Really Minorities?' (2012) 1 *Oxford Journal of Law and Religion* 57.

227 United Nations General Assembly. *Report of the Special Rapporteur on freedom of religion or belief, Heiner Bielefeldt*, 24 December 2012, A/HRC/22/51.

228 Ghanea 2012, 61.

229 Johannes Morsink, 'The Philosophy of the Universal Declaration' (1984) 6 *Human Rights Quarterly* 309.

230 Stephanie E. Berry, 'Bringing Muslim Minorities within the International Convention on the Elimination of All Forms of Racial Discrimination-Square Peg in a Round Hole?' (2011) 11 *Human Rights Law Review* 423; Brice Dickson, 'The United Nations and Freedom of Religion' (1995) 44 *The International and Comparative Law Quarterly* 327.

231 Malcolm D. Evans, 'Advancing Freedom of Religion or Belief: Agendas for Change' (2012) 1 *Oxford Journal of Law and Religion* 5.

unpredictable.[232] In the guidelines issued by the UN High Commissioner for Refugees to assist decision-makers in assessing religion-based asylum claims, "religion" denotes not only belief or identity, but also "way of life",[233] further complicating the relationship between the "religion" of the Refugee Convention and the "religion" of surrounding international legislation.

Similarly, the relationship between the "religion" of the UDHR and the "spiritual and religious traditions" of indigenous peoples protected under Article 12(1) in the UN Declaration on the Rights of Indigenous Peoples[234] is uncertain, not least due to the strong correlation between indigenous spirituality and religion and the rights of indigenous peoples to govern their own lands and be ruled by their own systems of laws.[235] In a related vein, the prohibition against "intentionally directing attacks against buildings dedicated to religion" in Article 8(2)(e)(iv) of the Statutes of the International Criminal Court is uncertain, both at the level of identifying "religious" buildings and in terms of the kinds of protections it may offer for individuals and communities affiliated with the concerned buildings.[236] More research is needed in order to provide a more comprehensive account of how legal regulations of religion at the international level interact and how they play out in domestic law. While the "freedom of religion or belief umbrella" has long dominated scholarly approaches to the concept of religion in international law,[237] the general expansion of legal regulations at the international level has led to the development of a

---

232 James C. Hathaway and Michelle Foster, *The Law of Refugee Status* (Cambridge University Press 2014).

233 UNHCR. *Guidelines on International Protection: Religion-Based Refugee Claims under Article 1A(2) of the 1951 Convention and/or the 1967 Protocol Relating to the Status of Refugees*, HCR/GIP/04/06, 28 April 2004.

234 United Nations General Assembly. *United Nations Declaration on the Rights of Indigenous Peoples*, A/RES/61/295, 13 September 2007.

235 Robin Perry, 'Balancing Rights or Building Rights? Reconciling the Right to Use Customary Systems of Law with Competing Human Rights in Pursuit of Indigenous Sovereignty' (2011) 24 *Harvard Human Rights Journal* 71; Siegfried Wiessner, 'Observations on the Human Rights Situation of Indigenous People in Nepal in Light of the UN Declaration on the Rights of Indigenous Peoples' (2008) 41 *Vanderbilt Journal of Transnational Law* 1141.

236 For an examination of how the article has been interpreted in a recent ICC case, see Juan-Pablo Pérez-León-Acevedo, 'International Criminal Justice Rendered Concerning the Attack against Timbuktu Mausoleums and Mosque: Focus on Religion-Related Considerations' (2017) 6 *Oxford Journal of Law and Religion* 180.

237 While Natan Lerner lists a limited number of additional instruments in his overview of the nature and minimum standards of the freedom of religion or belief, he does not address them in any detail, see Natan Lerner, 'The Nature and Minimum Standards of Freedom of Religion or Belief' (2000) *Brigham Young University Law Review* 906, 922–23.

large and growing body of international laws on religion that do not readily conform to the dictates of the freedom of religion or belief, and which should be made the subject of new studies in law and religion.

Third, the ideological stalemate following the Second World War effectively neutered the efforts to establish an international court for the monitoring of the incipient human rights framework. Instead, the monitoring of the large and growing body of international legal regulations of religion has fallen to a patchwork of committees and tribunals whose decisions are not formally binding under the principles of international law. The principal monitoring organs are ten human rights committees established as parts of international human rights treaties, the Universal Periodic Review (UPR) mechanism overseen by the UN Human Rights Council (UNHRC), and the Special Rapporteur on the Freedom of Religion or Belief, appointed under a mandate ratified by the UNHRC. While the special rapporteur mainly monitors the legal framework developed under the "freedom of religion or belief umbrella", the human rights committees and the UPR mechanism review the full spectrum of international human rights law. Additionally, international legal rules on religion beyond the "religion or belief umbrella" are monitored by the International Criminal Court, the International Court of Justice, several regional courts and international organizations like the International Labor Organization (ILO) and the UN Educational, Scientific and Cultural Organization (UNESCO). While some of these committees and courts cite one another in their regulatory approaches to religion, the majority do not, preferring to interpret their statutes in line with their primary regulatory purpose. As the number of legal regulations grows, their internal cohesion and the modes of their monitoring are likely to expand further, causing increased indeterminacy in the effects of regulation and adjudication.

Issues for Further Research

Drawing on this overview of how the expansion and differentiation of laws on religion has evolved and the many unresolved questions that arise from this evolution, we suggest that there is much to be gained for scholars working at the intersections between law and religion from a deeper engagement with the general mechanisms underlying legal change at the systemic level, drawing on insights from other fields of legal and socio-legal scholarship. While there is no reason to dismiss out of hand dominant themes in the scholarship on law and religion that frame legal change in relation to religion as unique or premised on the specific demographic changes taking place in the religious field, these hypotheses need to become subject to more rigorous analysis and testing. Additionally, scholarship on law and religion could connect with the wider field of legal scholarship by framing new research topics culled from foundational questions at the heart of legal theory, ranging from what the basic characteristics are of law and of the legal field, to the influence of legal indeterminacy, legal irritants and bureaucratization on the regulation of religion.

In addition to these foundational questions, which can be difficult to address in smaller, more limited case studies, we suggest that scholarship on law and religion could stand to benefit from a consideration of how their specific subject matter—be it a singular bill, an isolated court case or a theory of religious freedom—plays out across the different dimensions listed in the model developed by Blichner and Molander. This exercise would entail the questioning of what inspired the creation of the legal rule under examination (A/B), how these inspirations play out in relation to change in the erstwhile legal field (B), the extent to which the rule has generated or diminished conflict solving by recourse to law (C), whether it has expanded or curtailed the power of judges (D), and the extent to which it has helped provide a vocabulary for the self-conception and rights claims of social actors (E). These questions need not be part of the final product issued at the end of a completed case study, but could help sharpen the analytical focus at the beginning of new projects.

3C *Increased Conflict Solving by Recourse to Law*

As the scope of legal regulation expands and differentiates, the role of law as a tool to solve conflicts has grown, if not correspondingly, then at least with a degree of correlation. In the model suggested by Blichner and Molander, this growth can be broken down into three types. First, judicial conflict solving (C1) involves the formal legal system, drawing on established rules of procedure and qualified legal input. Second, legal conflict solving (C2) retains a connection with the legal framework, but takes place outside the formal legal system. Third, lay conflict solving (C3) takes place outside the legal system and the legal framework, with only a peripheral connection to the terms and concepts provided by the latter.[238]

The connection between the growth of legal regulations (see 3B) and increased conflict solving by recourse to law may seem self-evident, as the expansion and differentiation of legal regulations provide parties to conflicts with increasing numbers of tools with which to frame and litigate their claims. However, the growth of law can also have the opposite effect, as legislators develop legal frameworks that shut down the need for legal intervention, effectively causing the *dejuridification* of conflict solving. Additionally, the growth of legal regulations can also lead to decreased conflict solving by recourse to

238 Blichner and Molander 2008, 44.

law because of the increasing complexity and technicality of legal regulations, effectively limiting access to the legal system.

In tandem with the erstwhile growth in law as a tool and venue for the resolution of conflicts, the role of legal, judicial and lay conflict solving involving religion has increased over the last decades. This growth has been covered extensively in the literature on law and religion, where it constitutes one of the key impulses to the formation of the disciplinary field. However, the relation between this increase and (1) the general growth of legal conflict solving, (2) the relationship between its judicial, legal and lay dimensions, and (3) the instances where either of these dimensions have decreased have so far not been the subject of systematic or detailed analysis within the field. We suggest that a further appreciation of these aspects and their interrelationships may generate new and important insights and research questions for scholars working at the intersections of law and religion.

Solving Conflicts Related to Religion by Recourse to Law

Growing recourse to law in the resolution of conflicts shares the basic characteristics of growing legal regulation, forcing parties to conflicts to deal with legal indeterminacy, the growth of legal irritants and the increasing power of bureaucracies (see 3B). In particular, the widening reach of legislation coupled with the indeterminacy of the outcomes of conflict resolution procedures has inspired widespread *legal activism*, or *lawfare*, by which parties to a conflict utilize every available legal remedy to win their case. The paradigmatic case of legal activism is the litigation strategies developed by the anti-discrimination movement, which has been active in pushing both for the adoption of fresh legislation and for procedural fairness in court cases, fighting differential treatment of ethnic minorities, women, the disabled and sexual and gender minorities. This type of activism relies heavily on the process of "legal framing", whereby the legal framework provides the basic points of reference for the management of social relationships against the background of a shared legal order and culture of legality (see 3E).

Examples of legal activism to resolve conflicts involving religion are legion, ranging from the extensive litigation on religion before the ECtHR,[239] to the infamous apostasy and blasphemy cases that are rife in several Muslim majority countries,[240] and to the "strategic litigation" of marginal religious communities

239 Effie Fokas, 'Directions in Religious Pluralism in Europe: Mobilizations in the Shadow of European Court of Human Rights Religious Freedom Jurisprudence' (2015) 4 *Oxford Journal of Law and Religion* 54.

240 Agrama 2010.

like the Jehovah's Witnesses[241] and Scientology. Litigation and legal activism related to religion is not limited to international or statutory law, but can also be detected in constitutional law, as attested to by the large body of decisions on religion issued by the US Supreme Court and in numerous other jurisdictions (see also 3A).[242]

Due to the growing scope of laws that either regulate religion directly or expand the interface between the legal system and religious organizations and individuals, the spectrum of litigation related to religion is enormous, ranging from cases concerning the acceptable display of religious allegiances in the public sphere and the long and protracted attempts to prohibit dangerous sects or cults via efforts to secure similar access to the educational system for religious minorities, and to the autonomy of religious organizations in employment and discrimination law. These case types are only the tip of the iceberg of the vast number of issues that fall within the remit of a more narrowly construed concept of "religion law", as the fundamental indeterminacy of legislation that seeks to protect religious freedom or provide protection against religious discrimination generates religion-related litigation that requires a careful examination of existing precedent from domestic and international courts.

However, increased litigation on religion can also be found much farther afield, as the *bureaucratization* of laws that regulate religion lead to the determination of conflicts that are only peripherally or not at all attached to the provisions of religion law. These issues range far and wide, from the role of religion in the access to social benefits and specific rules governing religious exemptions from taxation, to the special status of religious buildings for conservation and the governance of sites that hold spiritual significance for indigenous peoples.

The broad nature of legal conflict resolution in questions relating to religion is partly due to the large and growing volume of available legal remedies, which provide conflicting parties with a variety of different options for litigation. While this connection is nonlinear, and may also result in the opposite effect, as legal change can result in the removal of monitoring bodies and special courts, the growth of remedies is likely to be related to the general growth of legal regulations (juridification B). The role of religion as an "irritant" that has

241 James T. Richardson and Pauline Côté, 'Disciplined Litigation, Vigilant Litigation, and Deformation: Dramatic Organizational Change in Jehovah's Witnesses' (2001) 40 *Journal for The Scientific Study of Religion* 11.

242 Leszek L. Garlicki, 'Perspectives on Freedom of Conscience and Religion in the Jurisprudence of Constitutional Courts' (2001) *Brigham Young University Law Review* 467.

travelled across a widening field of legal areas (see 3B) has brought the handling of religion to remedial institutions hitherto unfamiliar with religion as a part of their jurisdiction.

One example of this development is the role of religion in the caseload of mediation services, where "religion" can be part of the legal dispute, constitute an important backdrop for the claimants, be a core inspiration for the organizations that provide mediation services, or all of the above. Another example is the use of religious leaders in the preventive and rehabilitative work of law enforcement agencies, as mediators that may have better rapprochement with troubled youth from religious minorities. The "instrumental" role of religious leaders as mediators in conflict situations is not limited to local communities, but has also very much become an established feature of international diplomacy.

While the sheer number of these options can have a democratizing effect by providing multiple avenues for conflict resolution, the organizational, technical and economic conditions surrounding litigation can also serve to further entrench already deep-seated inequalities, which can be particularly harmful to the plight of religious minorities that are already vulnerable in other ways. One example of this effect is the recently intensified legal battle for increased religious autonomy in employment cases fought before the ECtHR, where religious organizations with a broad economic base stand a considerably stronger chance of winning through than smaller, less economically proficient organizations.[243] On the other hand side, the aftermath of the landmark *Employment Division v. Smith* (1990) decision of the US Supreme Court, where the ceremonial use of peyote by Native Americans was not given protection under the "free exercise" clause of the Constitution, unleashed a large-scale campaign to "restore" religious freedom, ultimately leading to the adoption of the federal Religious Freedom Restoration Act (RFRA, 1993) and a host of more expansive state-level RFRAs, some of which have been highly controversial. While these acts have done little to protect Native American religious exercise, they illustrate how legal change can also be instantiated as a result of litigation by non-privileged parties.

Moreover, recent years have also seen an increase in strategic funding being provided for non-privileged parties so that they can pursue litigation of high-profile symbolic issues first in the national courts and then in, for example,

243 Pasquale Annicchino, 'Winning the Battle by Losing the War: The Lautsi Case and the Holy Alliance between American Conservative Evangelicals, the Russian Orthodox Church and the Vatican to Reshape European Identity' (2011) 6 *Religion & Human Rights* 213.

the supranational court in Strasbourg in a bid to test and challenge prevailing interpretations of the limits to individual and collective religious autonomy.

Another aspect influencing the effects of litigation of religion is the risk of majoritarian bias in the judicial process, whose methodology and procedural rules for the determination of religion tend to rely on centuries of cultural hegemony and legal precedent tailor-made for majority traditions and their organizations. While this effect is likely to be higher for jurisdictions with strong ties between religion and state, it has also been identified in the case of the US, France and Turkey, all of which are textbook examples of different forms of religion/state "separationism". This bias can take the form of anything from judges leaning on their own "grab-bag" of theories of religion, via the hypotheses on the veracity of religious conversion provided by country experts in refugee status determination procedures, and to the applicability of religious or customary law to determine cases in the regular court system.

This majoritarian bias may not only be detected in the determination of what constitutes religion for legal purposes, but may equally well affect which conflicts end up with legal solutions (see below). While this is not unique to religion, but a general feature of how law and legal cultures provide differing options for litigation to different segments of society, the variance between actors within the "religious field" in their perception of the legitimacy and applicability of law as a tool for conflict resolution is likely to be more extensive than in the general population. One example of this difference can be attributed to some of the majoritarian biases identified above, as conflict resolution mechanisms like relationship counselling or child custody arbitration will tend to be developed with the needs of the majority population in mind, without being able to address the needs of religious minorities. However, resolving this issue can easily have equally damaging effects, as the development of "special interest" models of conflict resolution can trigger the "paradox of recognition" identified by Wendy Brown (see part 1).

Another example of how conflict resolution mechanisms cater differently to religious majorities and minorities is the trend among Western European states to stimulate the development of "representative" organs for the communities of religious minorities, in order to have a conversation partner for the resolution of social, political and legal conflicts relating to the communities in question. The generation of these organs has frequently led to infighting and conflicts, both within the organizations, between the organizations and the communities they are set to represent, and between the organizations and representatives of state authorities. As pointed out by Robert M. Cover, the moral, ethical and legal ties that bind communities are frequently not coextensive with, but contrast from and offer alternatives to those represented by state power, fundamentally altering their views of the capacity of law to resolve conflicts. In language reminiscent of the communitarian critique of liberalism offered by Alasdair MacIntyre, Cover stressed the "norm-generating aspects" of communities bound together by shared stories, experiences and traditions, inspiring normative commitments with authority far greater than that offered by state power.[244] While this effect has been subject to extensive previous research, its relationship to the overall growth in recourse to law in the resolution of conflicts has not been subject to systematic examination in the literature.

Judicial, Legal and Lay Conflict Solving Related to Religion

Because of the strong normative commitments maintained by the religious traditions that make up the communities that feature in the work of Cover and MacIntyre, conflicts related to religion frequently end up being resolved through "lay" forms of arbitration, in which religiously sanctioned norms constitute authoritative bodies of rules. Unlike the conception of lay conflict solving suggested by Blichner and Molander, however (see above), the rules and terms of procedure and opinion developed and maintained by religious communities do not happen in isolation from, or with a peripheral familiarity with the norms of the legal system, but frequently in opposition to and as an alternative to formal legal regulations. The role of such "lay" conflict solving is strongly divided across different religions and different jurisdictions, ranging from a role of religious courts as hardwired parts of legal regulation and adjudication, as in numerous states in the Middle East, and to their more informal and frequently controversial role in Western democracies, where religious forms of legal reasoning are often considered inherently suspect.[245] The importance of conflict resolution by recourse to religious laws demonstrates the narrow concept of "law" in the model developed by Blichner and Molander, whose terminological apparatus does not distinguish between the many different forms of lay conflict resolution that are available in modern nation states.

Importantly, the general growth of law as the principal arbiter of conflicts in society can not only be detected in increasing litigation and jurisprudence on religion in the formal legal system through legal activism and lawfare (see above), but may also be found in the reliance on legal frames of reference in public debates on religion, which have become thoroughly saturated with the terms and categories of law. Indeed, it would be hard to imagine the discussion

244 Robert M. Cover, 'The Supreme Court, 1982 Term Foreword: Nomos and Narrative' (1983) 97 *Harvard Law Review* 4, 32.

245 Ashe and Hélie 2014.

of any contentious religious conflict in society without reference to law, whose "fetishization" in late modern society has been described by John Comaroff as a turn towards "legal theology" in which law and legality gradually becomes sacralized (see also 3E).[246] While these discussions are largely pre-parliamentary and are led outside the confines of the formal legal system, their use of legal terms and categories establish a strong and vital connection both to adjudication in the formal legal system (C1) and, in the longer term, to the generation of new laws on religion (see 3B) and constitutional change (see 3A).

While some of these developments have been duly noted in previous research, we suggest that scholars of law and religion should pay greater attention to combinations between judicial (C1), legal (C2) and "lay" (C3) conflict solving related to religion, exploring the extent to which the large number of judicial procedures available under C1 and the fetishization of law under C2 serve to weaken or strengthen the appeal of lay conflict solving under C3, both in the sense suggested by Blichner and Molander, and in the more specific sense of "religious law" illustrated above. These combinations should not be limited to the conventional tropes of religion law, like religious freedom or anti-discrimination law (see 3B), but should be expanded to cover the full spectrum of interactions between law and religion: From the conceptions of religion operative in family law, whose vocabulary has been organically expanded to accommodate specific items of religious legislation on family relations,[247] to the role of "the religious" in the arbitration of contractual disputes, which are governed by the principle of party autonomy (*lex voluntatis*) in choosing legitimate norms,[248] the ways in which conflicts related to religion are resolved can rely on very different conceptions of the nature and scope of religion than the ones operative within more conventional religion law.

While these legal approaches are arguably peripheral to the majority of cases being decided under religion law in the conventional sense, they nevertheless constitute a part of the wider interaction between legal regulations and "religion", which in turn affect the wider "legal framing" of religion (see 3E). Adding these borderline cases to the vocabulary of law and religion scholars

---

246 John L. Comaroff, 'Reflections on the Rise of Legal Theology: Law and Religion in the Twenty-First Century' (2009) 53 *Social Analysis* 193.

247 Jane Mair, 'The Impact of Religion on European Family Law' in Jens M. Scherpe (ed), *European Family Law*, vol. 1 (Edward Elgar Publishing 2016) 294, 322.

248 Illias Bantekas, 'Freedom of Religion in Transnational Contract and Commercial Transactions' in Malcolm D. Evans, Peter Petkoff and Julian Rivers (eds), *The Changing Nature of Religious Rights under International Law* (Oxford University Press 2015) 286, 294.

may also provide additional rigor to the conceptual core of the discipline, as they serve to throw the "gray zone" at the outer limits of concept formation into sharper relief, which would seem to be a prerequisite for conceptually oriented scholarship.[249]

The Dejuridification of Conflict Solving Related to Religion

Although the overall growth of legal regulations would suggest a steady increase in litigation related to religion, they can also have the opposite effect. In particular, the growing emphasis on religious freedom as a fundamental right whose protection causes greater security and less conflict,[250] whose present "orphaned"[251] status is precarious and in need of greater attention across the trans-Atlantic divide,[252] is largely premised on the notion that any legal regulation of religion is detrimental to religious freedom as a basic human right. Hence, the principal manner in which religious freedom should be protected is not through increased legal protections or by additional remedial institutions, but by *dejuridifying* the determination of religion.

Indeed, this stance is shared across the spectrum of scholars working in the highly charged debate on religious freedom. On the one hand, from a critical, deconstructive perspective (see also part 2), scholars like Winnifred Fallers Sullivan and Elizabeth Shakman Hurd have observed how legal guarantees for religious freedom are "impossible" due to the "inherent violence"[253] of state law, which serve to render "invisible" the "diverse and multiform" religious practices that cannot or refuse to be assimilated into its normative frame.[254] From this perspective, then, the injection of "religion" into human rights treaties, constitutions and statutes should be evaded in its entirety. On the other hand, human rights scholars and activists working for increased respect for religious freedom internationally similarly view the legal determination of religion with suspicion, as "there is no generally agreed-upon definition of 'religion'",[255]

---

249 For a further discussion of the importance of identifying "gray zones", see James Mahoney and Gary Goertz, 'The Possibility Principle: Choosing Negative Cases in Comparative Research' (2004) 98 *The American Political Science Review* 653.

250 Brian J. Grim, 'Religious Freedom: Good for What Ails Us?' (2008) 6 *The Review of Faith & International Affairs* 3.

251 Mary-Ann Glendon, 'Is Religious Freedom an "Orphaned" Right?' in Evans, Petkoff and Rivers (eds) 2015, 1.

252 Knox Thames, 'Forging a Trans-Atlantic Partnership on Religious Freedom' (2014) 12 *The Review of Faith & International Affairs* 1.

253 Sullivan 2005, 158.

254 Hurd 2015, 55.

255 Lerner 2000, 930.

and any legal regulation that seeks to establish such definitions embark on "an extremely complicated question", requiring "a high degree of caution and diligence".[256] From this perspective, the removal of regulations on religion is not only desirable, but also serves to "increase the supply and activity of religion",[257] wherein religious choice is instantly stimulated by their escape from government control.

These calls for the dejuridification of religion have direct consequences for the capacity of legal rules and the judicial system to intervene and arbitrate in conflicts relating to religion: In a string of recent cases to come before the ECtHR, the question of the autonomy of religious organizations in labour disputes have been addressed by the court, in which religious organizations have successfully litigated on the limited jurisdiction of statutory law over "religious matters".[258] These calls for the dejuridification of regulations on the labour relations of religious organizations are not limited to the international level, but can also be found in a variety of domestic legal systems.[259]

A paradoxical side effect of the shared consensus among critics and caretakers of religious freedom that the regulation of religion should be avoided is the significant litigation and jurisprudence generated by constitutional or other overarching principles that guarantee a degree of autonomy or special status for distinct religious communities, their organizations and legal rules (see 3A). While these regulations have been adopted in order to safeguard different parts of "religion" from excessive encroachment by state-driven regulation and interference, they have provided a significant impetus for litigation that seeks to pin down the exact boundaries between state and religion. This effect is particularly noteworthy in the boom industry of scholarship tracking the different modes and modalities of "secularism",[260] where one of the central

256 Heiner Bielefeldt, 'Misperceptions of Freedom of Religion or Belief' (2013) 35 *Human Rights Quarterly* 33, 40.

257 Brian J. Grim, 'International Religion Indexes: Government Regulation, Government Favoritism, and Social Regulation of Religion' (2006) 2 *Interdisciplinary Journal of Research on Religion* 1.

258 Dominic McGoldrick, 'Religion and Legal Spaces—In Gods We Trust; in the Church We Trust, but Need to Verify' (2012) 12 *Human Rights Law Review* 759.

259 Pamela Slotte and Helge Årsheim, 'The Ministerial Exception—Comparative Perspectives', 4 *Oxford Journal of Law and Religion* 171.

260 For just a small tasting menu of this scholarship, see Rex Ahdar, 'Is Secularism Neutral?' (2013) 26 *Ratio Juris* 404; Talal Asad, 'Religion, Nation-State, Secularism' in Peter van der Veer and Hartmut Lehmann (eds), *Nation and Religion: Perspectives on Europe and Asia* (Princeton University Press 1999); Benjamin L. Berger, 'Belonging to Law: Religious

upshots appear to be the identification of "the active principle of secularism" as it plays out in different historical, cultural and political settings. According to Hussein Agrama, this principle entails that

> the state is authorized to distinguish between the "civil" and "religious" dimensions of an act, and on that basis decide whether the act is enforceable, punishable, or otherwise deserving of protection or exemption under the law. And that process always involves often-unarticulated understandings about what religion in the abstract is, or should be. Hence, the state is always drawing a line between the religious and the secular, and reserving its sole authority to do so.[261]

Because of the active principle of secularism, the complete dejuridification of religion appears to be a chimera: the primary means by which "religion", in whatever guise, can be shielded from state incursions and sanctions intended either to protect or foster the role of religion in society is through its legal regulation, which inevitably forces legislators and adjudicators to determine "religion" in some way or form. In this way, the wishes of critics and caretakers of religious freedom alike to preserve a non-legal space where "religion" can thrive unbridled from legal regulations tend to end up in the "paradox of recognition" identified by Wendy Brown (see above), through which efforts to shield certain sectors of society from differential treatment end up reifying and sharpening the boundaries of those sectors (see above). Hence, the dejuridification of religion, understood as the decrease in regulation and litigation on religion, is first and foremost available through legal recognition (juridification A and B), which again tends to cause increased litigation (juridification C), and possibly also the growing power of judges (juridification D).

Difference, Secularism, and the Conditions of Civic Inclusion' (2014) 24 *Social and Legal Studies* 47; Effie Fokas, 'Secularism and Secularity: Contemporary International Perspectives' (2010) 11 *Culture and Religion* 163; Elizabeth Shakman Hurd, 'The Political Authority of Secularism in International Relations' (2004) 10 *European Journal of International Relations* 235; Ahmet T. Kuru, 'Passive and Assertive Secularism: Historical Conditions, Ideological Struggles, and State Policies toward Religion' (2011) 59 *World Politics* 568; Saba Mahmood, 'Secularism, Hermeneutics, and Empire: The Politics of Islamic Reformation' (2006) 18 *Public Culture* 323; Arvind Pal-Mandair and Markus Dressler (eds), *Secularism and Religion-Making* (Oxford University Press 2011); Rivers 2010.

261 Agrama 2010, 503.

Issues for Further Research

This mapping exercise has teased out a number of tensions and ambiguities that could be further explored by scholars working at the intersections between law and religion. Most importantly, scholars working with the resolution of religious conflicts should be challenged to formulate case studies that are sensitive to the multiple, frequently overlapping avenues of litigation available to the parties in a conflict. The availability of remedies can have a decisive influence on every aspect of a conflict, from its resolution and precedent and down to its very formulation.

Moreover, the ways in which different remedial institutions at the international and domestic level interact, and the extent to which their mandates overlap or even contradict one another, these aspects should become part of the scholarly analysis. Parsing forms of conflict solving into judicial, legal and lay forms also helps sharpen the analytical rigor of research questions, and should be a natural part of research into how religious conflicts become subject to legal regulation and adjudication. Finally, researching the resolution of religious conflicts also necessitates the examination of the ways in which such conflict resolution mechanisms interact with the growth of law (A/B), the power of the judiciary (D) and the tendency to frame social issues on the background of a common legal order (E).

3D *Increased Judicial Power*

What law applies to a particular situation and case? How should a specific piece of legislation be interpreted and understood? When these kinds of questions arise and there is uncertainty about how to answer them, the spotlight is turned to adjudicators. The more uncertainty there is, the more discretionary power is vested in those appointed to administer justice (as well as others holding legal expertise). Such is also the case when legal rules for various reasons are exceedingly inaccessible to the general public and citizens have a hard time making sense of the laws.[262]

262 Blichner and Molander 2008, 45: "A fourth meaning of juridification refers to increased judicial power. Given certain judicial competencies, the main sources of this power are law's indeterminacy and/or lack of transparency. Indeterminacy generally means that it is difficult to determine the state of the law relevant to a particular case, from the point of view of the jurisprudential community. Transparency generally refers to the degree of openness and intelligibility of law, from the citizens' point of view. The most extreme case of 'judicial' power is where there are no common legal rules and a third party has absolute competency to judge in cases of conflict."

Blichner and Molander talk about these two features as law's indeterminacy and lack of transparency and their fourth dimension of juridification stands for the increase of judicial power which these two features yield. "[I]ndeterminacy and lack of transparency increase the importance and dependence on legal advice and in-court settlement", they note. For, "when transparency decreases, it increases the power of those that master the difficulties relative to those that do not".[263] Other scholars have sought to capture this phenomenon in terms of *judicialisation*,[264] *juristocracy* or *courtocracy* as discussed in the introduction as well as above in part 3B, and in so doing have reflected also in various ways on the other dimensions A, B and C of juridification. Juridification processes in these other dimensions may increase or decrease juridification D:[265]

> According to our definition of judicial power (juridification D), juridification A, B and C may yield judicial power insofar as this increases indeterminacy or reduces transparency. More generally speaking, judicial power stems from lack of transparency and indeterminacy when it comes to the legal doctrines involved, the interpretive operations involved and the application of law.[266]

Hence, depending on the legislative action taken at the level of constitutional or statutory law, judicial power may grow. This is so because specification of particular laws at these levels does not necessarily lessen the need for interpretation, but also because a considerable increase and diversification of norms (see 3B) in and of itself may fuel the bewilderment of the addressees of the laws.[267] Moreover, it is understandable that increased conflict-solving with

---

263 Blichner and Molander 2008, 45.

264 Blichner and Molander here refer to C. Neal Tate and Torbjorn Vallinder, *The Global Expansion of Judicial Power* (New York University Press 1995); Alec Stone Sweet, 'Judicialisation and the Construction of Governance' in Martin Shapiro and Alec Stone Sweet (eds), *On Law, Politics and Judicialisation* (Oxford University Press 2002) 71; and Joakim Nergelius, 'North and South: Can the Nordic States and the European Continent Find Each Other in the Constitutional Area—or are They Too Different?' in Martin Scheinin (ed), *Welfare State and Constitutionalism—Nordic Perspectives* (Nordic Council of Ministers 2001).

265 Blichner and Molander 2008, 45.

266 Blichner and Molander 2008, 45; referring further to Brian Leiter and Jules L. Coleman, 'Determinacy, Objectivity and Authority' (1994) 142 *University of Pennsylvania Law Review* 549, 559.

267 Lars C. Blichner, 'Juridification from Below: The Dynamics of MacCormick's Institutional Theory of Law' in Augustín J. Menéndez and John E. Fossum (eds), *Law and Democracy*

reference to law as such (see 3C) may increase the relative power of adjudicators and other legal experts. However, the nature and practice of law per se is also important:

> Most would accept that the law should live up to some standards of transparency and determinacy, and most would agree that some level of indeterminacy and lack of transparency is a fact of law. The main disagreement concerns to what degree this amounts to judicial power in the sense of juridification D, and what the limits to the exercise of this power are, while still holding on to a concept of rule of law. Much of the disagreement hinges on what properly belongs to the class of legal reasons.[268]

Hence, underlining law's indeterminacy is not per se necessarily a critical remark. Instead, it amounts to making an observation about an intrinsic quality of law (see 3B). Indeed, it is worth exploring in a bit more detail possible ways in which indeterminacy may be seen as a feature—and indeed an inherent feature—of law.

Indeterminacy as a Feature of Law

Drawing on Lawrence Rosen, and others, we could say that beyond addressing disputes that arise and regulate social life, law is "a species of social imagination"[269] and will shape our vision of the world around us. What we encounter is a way of making sense of the world. Translated to the terms of this article: through processes of juridification matters become legally framed in particular ways. Some things will stand forth as matters of concern, while the significance of other things will be downplayed. International lawyer Martti Koskenniemi has identified this, in a context where he speaks of human rights, as one of the ways in which such rights are the outcome of politics. We are dealing with a "process whereby an aspect of reality becomes characterised in terms of rights".[270] Laws are the outcomes of "political processes" also in the related sense that their final formulations and content are the result of negotiation and compromise. Nowhere is this as true as with regard to international treaties, but we can equally think about processes of legislation taking place in national parliaments here.

---

in Neil MacCormick's Legal and Political Theory: The Post-Sovereign Constellation, Law and Philosophy Library vol. 93 (Springer 2011) 27, 44.

268 Blichner and Molander 2008, 45–46.

269 Lawrence Rosen, *Law as Culture* (Princeton University Press 2006) 8–9, 11–12.

270 Martti Koskenniemi, *The Politics of International Law* (Hart Publishing, 2011) 157.

Moreover, and as noted in part 3B, knowing that you cannot possibly discern in advance all the future scenarios that you may reasonably want to regulate, i.e. the *precise* scope of a particular law, phrasings will have to be general and open enough to accommodate the unforeseen, at least to some extent. Hence, returning to Blichner and Molander's remarks above: While in keeping with the principle of legality it is reasonable to expect of "adequate" laws that they are accessible and intelligible so that not only the jurisprudential community, but also lay persons may have a reasonable idea of when, where and how they apply, laws can seldom be so exhaustively formulated as to never give rise to questions pertaining to their application or meaning. Therefore, we cannot exclude judicial power, nor does it seem like a very sensible thing to always pursue this. Indeed, as Blichner points out in a single-authored piece: in some areas of law you may want to define very strictly the competence of those holding adjudicative power, whereas in other areas of law context sensitivity is key to decision-making and consequently discretionary power crucial.[271]

Koskenniemi has also repeatedly underlined how the power of decision-making is an inescapable feature given the indeterminacy of law. To him, indeterminacy stands for several things—human rights, for instance, are formulated in "open-ended language" that not only invites, but necessitates interpretation. Moreover, conditionality is built into human rights law given that human rights as legal rights always come accompanied with exceptions, limitations and derogation clauses, the scope of which is "never clearly defined".[272] When should you apply the right or the exception? According to Koskenniemi, there is no fixed point in law to which we could appeal so as to escape this ultimate need to make a decision. There is always room left for discretionary power.

Lastly, and related to this, the interpreters of the law are institutions with various commitments that affect the kinds of decisions that are made. Ultimately, someone always has to make the concrete decisions and this is linked to value choices and the subjective assessment of the "evidence" of the case. Returning to Koskenniemi, in the case of determining the scope of a right in light of possible exceptions and limitations, "the scope of rights becomes conditioned by choices that seem justifiable only be references to alternative conceptions of the good society".[273] While international law may be a classic case of this, constitutional norms are equally prone to generalizing formulations, whose more detailed interpretation is then left to the national legislator

271 Blichner 2011, 45.

272 Koskenniemi 2011, 158.

273 Koskenniemi 2011, 159. Hence, we should shy away from "de-politicizing" law.

(leading to juridification B) and/or the judiciary (leading to juridification D). Even quite specific pieces of legislation do not necessarily do away with the space or need for interpretation.

In fact, we could also claim that the alternative—no discretionary power—would be disastrous in and of itself. Or as Jan Klabbers recently put this point more generally with regard to the idea of the rule of law: the rule of law is meant to preclude "the arbitrary Rule of man but cannot mean that no men and women are involved to begin with and should not be involved".[274] In fact, "the Rule of Law requires interjection by people, not least in interpreting and applying the law."[275] Hence, what we (should) desire is that those who do occupy crucial positions of power have certain qualities and competences so that law does not become simply "a sheer tool of domination",[276] and all the more so in cases where application of the law rises about the minimal threshold of routine.

Of course, this hints at a broader discussion that lies beyond the scope of this article, but the point that we wish to make here concerns the need to recognize "the role of human agency".[277] This is also embedded in the larger question of judicial power raised by Blichner and Molander, who distinguish between "potential judicial power" and "judicial power in action".[278] While the former refers to the necessity of "some level of indeterminacy and lack of transparency is a fact of law",[279] the *actual* use of judicial power may both increase and decrease indeterminacy and transparency: Judicial interpretation may limit the scope of possible meanings[280] of a particular legal rule. This then also may amount to de-juridification D to a certain extent, given that some interpretations are ruled out and meaning is "closed down", so to say.

---

274 Jan Klabbers, 'Doing Justice? Bureaucracy, the Rule of Law and Virtue Ethics' (2017) 6 *Rivista di Filosofia di Diritto* 27, 28–29.

275 Klabbers 2017, 29.

276 Quote from Klabbers 2017, 30, who in turn cites Gianluigi Palombella, 'The Rule of Law at Home and Abroad' (2016) 8 *Hague Journal on the Rule of Law* 1, 2.

277 Quote from Klabbers 2017, 31. See Klabbers 2017 for one exploration of what "virtuous adjudication" could be taken to entail.

278 Blichner and Molander 2008, 46.

279 For just one other illustrious voice making the same remark as regards the inherent indeterminacy of legal rules, see H.L.A. Hart, *The Concept of Law* (Clarendon 1961) 124–25.

280 Blichner and Molander 2008, 45–46. "[T]he more interpretations made the less room there is for further interpretation given that there is a limit to the number of interpretations that may be made". Blichner and Molander 2008, 46.

Simultaneously, depending on the new doctrine of law established, it can actually increase judicial power too.[281]

> In general terms, 'local' processes of juridification and dejuridification D may alternate depending on factors such as the determinacy of new doctrines and laws, the tendency on the part of the judiciary to make new and possibly innovative interpretations and the number of interpretations actually carried out.[282]

This process interacts with the other dimensions of juridification, as the production of new doctrines of law, which takes place when "interpretations made are established as doctrines of law", may trigger legislative changes. It may also affect concrete dealings with larger society as it turns to law and judicial bodies for the purpose of solving conflicts.

> This implies juridification A or B, and may be affected by juridification C. Juridification D relates to A when interpretive power is used to establish or change constitutive rules and principles. Juridification D relates to juridification B when interpretative power is used to refine a particular law. Juridification D relates to juridification C when interpretative power is used to reject a case.[283]

Adding to this set of observations: what is indeed "religion"? The indeterminacy of the phenomenon that we seek to regulate legally adds to the complexity of the processes already accounted for (see 3B). We also touched upon this matter shortly in part 2 above, where we noted that the amorphous nature of the phenomenon of religion and the fluidity of religious identities and communities has led some scholars to question the reasonableness of religious freedom legislation as such. Part of this critique is directed exactly against the discretionary space that adjudicators in consequence are permitted in matters of religion and the way this affects adjudication in a detrimental fashion.

The way meaning is "closed down", the critics claim, correlates with the prejudices and preconceptions of the adjudicators themselves, rendering certain claims to religious freedom legally unintelligible, most often those that in some way or the other present a challenge to familiar and majoritarian patterns of religion. Hence, religion law and adjudication on its basis is complicit

281 Blichner and Molander 2008, 46.

282 Blichner and Molander 2008, 46.

283 Blichner and Molander 2008, 46 (fn. 49).

in processes of *otherization*. As Winnifred Fallers Sullivan, Elizabeth Shakman Hurd, Saba Mahmood and Peter G. Danchin emphatically state in the introduction to their edited volume on the *Politics of Religious Freedom*:

> Today the word religion brings together a vast and diverse, even shifting, set of social and cultural phenomena that no longer convincingly underwrite and justify legal action in its name. To continue to use the word in law is to invite discrimination.[284]

Furthermore, with regard to legal framing (juridification E, see below), the authors point out that distortion of religious identities takes place as individuals and communities seek to conform to the parameters of "legal religion" and "social realities" are translated into "legal categories".[285] The terminology they use to capture various aspects of what we here call processes of juridification of religion is "legalization of religion".[286]

Increased Judicial Power over "Religion Law"

In their article 'Regulation of "Religion" and the "Religious": The Politics of Judicialization and Bureaucratization in India and Indonesia', Yüksel Sezgin and Mirjam Künkler note how the rulers both in colonial and postcolonial religiously heterogeneous India readily outsourced dispute resolution in religious matters to courts.[287] Likewise, Clark B. Lombardi and Nathan J. Brown have pointed out that the constitutional juridification of religion including "religious law" (juridification A) that has taken place in Egypt, and the general language in which it has proclaimed that "the principles of Islamic sharia" are to be "the main source of legislation", has transferred power over religion and "religious law" to the country's Supreme Constitutional Court, a task in which the court has exhibited independence.[288] Also, in his recent article "Singing

284 Sullivan et al. 2015, 7. As seen above, discrimination could, of course, be seen as an inevitable feature of law.

285 Sullivan et al. 2015, 8.

286 Sullivan et al. 2015, 8.

287 Yüksel Sezgin and Mirjam Künkler, 'Regulation of "Religion" and the "Religious": The Politics of Judicialization and Bureaucratization in India and Indonesia' (2014) 52 *Comparative Studies in Society and History* 448, 450.

288 Clark B. Lombardi and Nathan J. Brown, 'Do Constitutions Requiring Adherence to Shari'a threaten Human Rights? How Egypt's Constitutional Court Reconciles Islamic Law with the Liberal Rule of Law' (2006) 21 *American University International Law Review* 379; Clark B. Lombardi and Nathan J. Brown, 'Islam in Egypt's New Constitution' (*Foreign*

from the Same Hymn Sheet? What the Differences between the Strasbourg and Luxembourg Courts Tell Us about Religious Freedom, Non-Discrimination, and the Secular State", Ronan McCrea notes how "Pan-European courts have become an increasingly important focus of disputes in this area in recent times."[289]

Here, we explore the ECtHR in Strasbourg, in order to exemplify how despite the increasing extent and differentiation of "religion law", the nature and scope of these laws is radically indeterminate, inviting a considerable increase in judicial power. One place where this is heartfelt is in the jurisprudence on Article 9. To start with, the European Convention for the Protection of Human Rights and Fundamental Freedoms (ECHR) forms part of a canon of legal and non-legally binding human rights instruments which Nehal Bhuta has called "a bricolage of rights forms derived from heterogeneous traditions and specific political projects".[290] Besides, the language which following such a complex process of juridification B can be found in Article 9 is open-ended:

> 1. Everyone has the right to freedom of thought, conscience and religion; this right includes freedom to change his religion or belief and freedom, either alone or in community with others and in public or private, to manifest his religion or belief, in worship, teaching, practice and observance.
> 2. Freedom to manifest one's religion or beliefs shall be subject only to such limitations as are prescribed by law and are necessary in a democratic society in the interests of public safety, for the protection of public order, health or morals, or for the protection of the rights and freedoms of others.

Policy, 13 December 2012) University of Washington School of Law Research Paper No. 2013–19, 1 <https://ssrn.com/abstract=2258252> accessed 15 June 2017. See also e.g. Hirschl 2006, 721.

Lombardi and Brown also account for the political bargaining and compromise that accompanied the work on the new draft Constitution of Egypt from 2012, and which goes to confirm observations made by Koskenniemi earlier in this section.

289 Ronan McCrea, 'Singing from the Same Hymn Sheet? What the Differences between the Strasbourg and Luxembourg Courts Tell Us about Religious Freedom, Non-Discrimination, and the Secular' (2016) 5 *Oxford Journal of Law and Religion* 183.

290 Bhuta 2014, 10. For a new study that revisits this development as regards the European human rights system and the ECHR in general, see Duranti 2017. Of course, also other articles of the ECHR in combination with Article 9 or without are crucial when we narrow in on the convention as part of "religion law".

Notions like public order, health or morals are inherently indeterminate, warranting interpretation and empowering the judicial body in question.[291] However, while the norms themselves are open-ended, the gradual development of legal doctrines also affect the practice of interpretation and the space and limits of possible interpretations, giving contours and direction to judicial power and discretion. How does this play out in the context of European human rights law on religion?

Certain key concepts and notions as regards religion inform European human rights law and jurisprudence and contribute to how authority is allocated, conflicts resolved, cases framed and religious identities constructed. Summing up observations made by a number of scholars throughout the years of existence of the ECtHR we could say that in the court, religion is both considered to be a largely private matter and the object of sovereign control, "de-juridified" and not.

This means that the legal articulation of religion developed at the court simultaneously protects religion, affects it, and makes sure that states can make certain inroads to the sphere of the religious when need be. As stated in the landmark case of *Kokkinakis* v. *Greece* from 1993, the following sentences spell out something akin to "general principles", which is also how the judgment itself phrases it:

> 31. As enshrined in Article 9 (art. 9), freedom of thought, conscience and religion is one of the foundations of a "democratic society" within the meaning of the Convention. It is, in its religious dimension, one of the most vital elements that go to make up the identity of believers and their conception of life, but it is also a precious asset for atheists, agnostics, sceptics and the unconcerned. The pluralism indissociable from a democratic society, which has been dearly won over the centuries, depends on it.
>
> While religious freedom is primarily a matter of individual conscience, it also implies, inter alia, freedom to "manifest [one's] religion". Bearing witness in words and deeds is bound up with the existence of religious convictions.
>
> According to Article 9 (art. 9), freedom to manifest one's religion is not only exercisable in community with others, "in public" and within the

291 The setup of Article 9 also typifies a point that Koskenniemi makes with regard to indeterminacy, namely that rights adjudicators have to choose between applying the rule or the exception: either you affirm that there is a right to freedom of religion or belief in a particular case, or you conclude that this right can justifiably be limited.

> circle of those whose faith one shares, but can also be asserted "alone" and "in private"; ....
> 33. ... recognises that in democratic societies, in which several religions coexist within one and the same population, it may be necessary to place restrictions on this freedom in order to reconcile the interests of the various groups and ensure that everyone's beliefs are respected.[292]

These sentences have been reproduced almost verbatim in case law ever since. Malcolm Evans recently called it a "mantra" of sorts.[293] We find expressed here certain values and principles that solidify the future interpretation of Article 9: Religion in a multitude of forms is intrinsic to the democratic society which is cherished and which one seeks to protect. Yet, despite this seemingly accommodating vision, and the fact that the ECtHR in principle does not want to say what is or is not religion, nor rule on the legitimacy of different beliefs, we also catch a glimpse of a normative articulation of religion and religious freedom, and of conceptual presuppositions and deep structures of the legal framework, which affects the way life, freedom and equality in matters of faith are currently legally imagined and the boundaries envisioned for such freedom.

That limits have to be put to legal rights is clear. The point of raising this matter here, is to draw attention to how line-drawing of this kind and the working out of the concrete content of religious freedom involves allocation of authority and can lead to increased or alternatively decreased judicial power at national levels and with regard to the ECtHR itself. While paragraph 2 formulates the premises for when States may justifiably interfere with a person's freedom to manifest his or her faith as the demand for a legitimate aim and a legal basis for the interference, the interference must also be proportionate to the legitimate aim pursued.

With regard to ECHR Article 10, Klabbers has pointed out that: "The problem with a proportionality analysis, any proportionality analysis, is that it is never clear in advance which terms are to be entered into the equation."[294] We could assume that this observation also holds relevance in regard to Article 9. Transparency may be undercut by the way it to some extent remains open to

---

292 *Kokkinakis* v. *Greece*, Appl. No. 14307/88, 25 May 1993, paras. 31, 33.

293 Malcolm Evans, presentation on 'The Freedom of Religion or Belief in the ECHR since *Kokkinakis* Or 'Quoting *Kokkinakis*'', at Expert Conference on "The European Court of Human Rights and the Freedom of Thought, Conscience and Religion: The 25-Year Legacy of Kokkinakis," 27–28 May 2017 at Central European University in Budapest, 27 May 2017, on file with the authors.

294 Klabbers 2017, 37.

both the national judiciary, and after that the ECtHR, how it will construe the case and the interests, needs and rights that it will subject to a proportionality analysis. Adding to the complexity of the matter, the ECtHR has developed the doctrine of "margin of appreciation" which considers national authorities best placed to carry out said proportionality analysis and determine whether or not a limitation of a right is necessary and in accordance with the ECHR.[295] Returning to part 3B, what we encounter here could be viewed also in terms of a lens through which to resolve the acceptable travel patterns of legal concepts and norms.

Drawing on the work of Susanna Mancini, Effie Fokas relates the doctrine of margin of appreciation to the need to mediate the universal assertions of human rights with the principle of subsidiarity which is central to the ECHR too:

> The principle of subsidiarity (in fact a religious-originated—Roman Catholic—concept suggesting that a matter ought to be handled by the smallest, lowest, or least centralized authority capable of addressing the matter effectively), is a fundamental aspect of the ECHR. In the ECtHR context, the principle dictates that while certain standards must be universally observed by all contracting states, each contracting state is, in the first place, responsible for securing the rights and freedoms protected by the convention. According to Mancini, the Court developed the doctrine of the 'margin of appreciation' to reconcile the potential tension between universality and subsidiarity.[296]

However, as Kristin Henrard has observed: depending on the specific issue, there is considerable variation with regard to the margin of appreciation afforded to states. Among other things it depends on whether or not a "European consensus" is detectable as regards the specific matter, which in turn reflects [the

---

295 A key case for the formulation of this doctrine is a case under article 10, *Handyside v. United Kingdom*, where: "The Court points out that the machinery of protection established by the Convention is subsidiary to the national systems safeguarding human rights. The Convention leaves to each Contracting State, in the first place, the task of securing the rights and freedoms it enshrines." *Handyside* v. *United Kingdom*, Appl. No. 5493/72, 7 December 1976, para. 32.

296 Fokas 2015, 58; Susanna Mancini, 'The Crucifix Rage: Supranational Constitutionalism Bumps against the Counter-Majoritarian Difficulty' (2010) 6 *European Constitutional Law Review* 6, 20–21.

ECtHR's] "concern for its own legitimacy in relation to the contracting states".[297] If a European consensus is considered to exist, states have less space to maneuver. Moreover, even if the margin of appreciation is mentioned, it does not per definition mean that the ECtHR would not carry out a "strict scrutiny" of the facts of the case.[298] As a sign of constitutive juridification A we can take the fact that this doctrine, which developed out of case law, recently found recognition in Article 1 of Protocol No 15 to the ECHR.[299]

Hernard's observations are insightful in regard to cases dealing with matters pertaining to religion, regarding which the ECtHR has repeatedly stated that: "where questions concerning the relationship between State and religions are at stake, questions on which opinion in a democratic society may reasonably differ widely, the role of the national decision-making body must be given special importance".[300] Hence, the margin of appreciation affords states leeway when it comes to determining the proper scope of national "religion law" according to their own specific contextual constraints. While this allows legislatures to reach a more firmly established basis for their laws on religion, it is worth underlining in the context of this article that a practical effect is frequently also one of allowing considerable autonomy to domestic judiciaries.

To give an example: In cases that have concerned so-called religious employers who for various reasons have terminated or not renewed a contract of an employee, the ECtHR has found that states have a positive duty under the ECHR to ensure employees the opportunity "to have a decision that concerns the terms of employment and its possible termination examined by a court of law".[301] When such cases subsequently have been brought before the ECtHR, it has scrutinized the actions of the states and sought to ascertain whether the employees in question have had the possibility to submit their cases for review by public authorities and have national courts struck a fair balance between the rights, freedoms and interests of employees and religious employers.[302] Yet

297 Kristin Henrard, 'How the European Court of Human Rights' Concern Regarding European Consensus Tempers the Effective Protection of Freedom of Religion (2015) 4 *Oxford Journal of Law and Religion* 398, 400.

298 Henrard 2015, 413.

299 For a discussion of Protocol No 15, see e.g. Dean Spielmann, 'Whither the Margin of Appreciation' (2014) 67 *Current Legal Problems* 49.

300 *Schüth* v. *Germany*, App. No. 162/03, 23 September 2010, para 58. See also e.g. *Leyla Şahin* v. *Turkey* [GC], App. No. 44774/98, para 109.

301 Slotte and Årsheim 2015, 180–81.

302 See e.g. *Schüth* v. *Germany*, para. 67, *Siebenhaar* v. *Germany*, App. No. 18136/02, 3 February 2011, para. 45; *Sindicatul "Păstorul cel Bun"* v. *Romania* [GC], App. No. 2330/09, 9 July 2013, para. 159.

the ECtHR has simultaneously affirmed that states enjoy "a certain margin of appreciation" as regards the matters at hand.[303] The emphasis on balancing different sets of rights in such religion related cases points to the inherent indeterminacy of European human rights law and lessens the transparency of legal decision making, whose technical vocabulary is most readily accessible to legal expertise.

On the whole, the way the ECtHR has operationalized the margin of appreciation has had the effect of both increasing and decreasing its own judicial power. We can find an example of this in the case of *Lautsi and Others* v. *Italy*, a case that attracted what Fokas has called "unprecedented interest".[304] The ECtHR had to decide whether or not it amounted to a human rights violation that Italian state school classrooms were adorned with crucifixes. Without entering into the details of the case here,[305] in 2009 the first instance Second Section chamber ruled in favour of the applicant, Ms Lautsi, holding that there had been a violation of Article 2 of Protocol No 1 taken together with Article 9. The ECtHR concluded that the Italian state had not remained impartial and neutral but instead had sided with a particular majority religion in a way that violated the right of parents to have their religious or philosophical convictions respected in the education of their children.

Many observers found this first Lautsi judgment a "natural" corollary of the previous reasoning of the ECtHR, which for some time had sided, increasingly so, with those who found that equal treatment in matters of faith and respect for religious diversity required that one cuts all ties between state and religion and minimize the influence of religion over public and political life. A secularizing agenda had shone through in the decision-making of the ECtHR, above all in cases dealing with Islam. It addressed constitutive juridification of religion (see 3A) with the aim of limiting the power of states over religion and vice versa and it questioned preferential state treatment of some religions.[306]

303 *Schüth* v. *Germany*, para. 55.

304 Fokas 2015, 62.

305 *Affaire Lautsi* c. *Italie*, Requête n° 30814/06, 3 novembre 2009; *Lautsi and Others* v. *Italy* [GC], App. No. 30814/06, 18 March 2011. See also e.g. the various articles in Jeroen Temperman (ed), *The Lautsi Papers: Multidisciplinary Reflections on Religious Symbols in the Public School Classroom* (Martinus Nijhoff Publishers 2012).

306 For a discussion of trends and secularist tendencies in ECtHR jurisprudence, see e.g. Fokas 2015, 61; Matthias Koenig, 'Governance of Religious Diversity at the ECHR' in Jane Bolden and Will Kymlincka (eds), *International Approaches to the Governance of Ethnic Diversity* (Oxford University Press 2012); Sylvie Langlaude, 'Indoctrination, Secularism, Religious Liberty, and the ECHR' (2006) 55 *International & Comparative Law Quarterly* 929; Julie Ringelheim, 'Du voile au crucifix: La neutralité de l'état dans la jurisprudence

The Chamber judgment was both celebrated and the object of severe criticism; for confounding neutrality and secularism,[307] for meddling in things that were ultimately the states' own business and for negating centuries of history.[308] It was overturned in the subsequent Grand Chamber judgment in 2011 in which the ECtHR sided with the defendant, the Italian state. While still affirming the foundational values and principles of religious pluralism, neutrality and so forth, and responding to critics by stating that secularism was, in fact, one life-view among others, the ECtHR assessed differently the facts of the case and transferred more clearly the principal interpretative prerogative and hence power and authority to the state. Actually, while the margin of appreciation is mentioned only 3 times in the Chamber judgment—by the defending state—in the Grand Chamber judgment, the margin of appreciation is referred to a staggering 27 times, out of which 8 times in the ECtHR's own concluding remarks.[309] Hence, while the second Lautsi judgment does not refute religious pluralism, it strengthens the power of states to interpret its scope and content (interpretative subsidiarity). With Blichner and Molander, we can say that the ECtHR here, through its interpretation, limits its own judicial power by reference to the doctrine of margin of appreciation.[310]

There have since been cases like *S.A.S.* v. *France*, where the applicant sought to challenge the French blanket ban on full face coverings in public places. Reading through this judgment and the argumentation up to the very last part of the judgment, it comes across as if the person in question has framed her case and identity in a way that matches the articulation of religion and personhood that the European human rights framework puts forth. It ticks the boxes for "sound" argumentation in matters of faith and the role of religion in a democratic society from the Strasbourg perspective under Article 9. And the ECtHR

de la Cour Européenne des Droits de l'Homme' [From Veils to Crucifix: State Neutrality in the Case Law of the European Court of Human Rights] (2014) Cridho Working Paper 2014/1, <https://ssrn.com/abstract=2459454> or <http://dx.doi.org/10.2139/ssrn.2459454> accessed 13 June 2017.

307 Fokas 2015, 65.

308 The critique of judicialisation and judicial review as counter-majoritarian is of course familiar from other contexts too and not exclusive to the European human rights system. For a discussion, see e.g. ECtHR Hirschl 2004; Hirschl 2006.

309 Fokas 2015, 66. In the subsequent cases of *Sindicatul 'Păstorul cel bun'* v. *Romania*, *Fernandéz Martínez* v. *Spain* and *S.A.S.* v. *France*, the same trend continues with 9 and 12 and 10 references each. Fokas 2015, 66. Fokas notes that the ECtHR returns from a narrowed margin of appreciation to broader one. Fokas 2015, 62.

310 Blichner and Molander 2008, 46.

does to a large extent acknowledge its own authority over the matter and that there are limits to the margin of appreciation afforded to states. Moreover, it does not accept some of the arguments that states have previously successfully used in similar cases.

Yet, simultaneously the ECtHR adopts a "new" legal concept called "living together", from the French context. It ends up still siding with the respondent state against the applicant, finding that it was legitimate to restrict the right to wear a full-face veil in public in order to protect other people's rights; in this case, the "right of others to live in a space of socialisation which makes living together easier".[311] Moreover, the ECtHR reasons that states have a wide margin of appreciation when it comes to the ways in which social interaction is promoted.

We can take this new legal concept as an example of what Klabbers observed above concerning openness as to the terms that end up in the balance in a proportionality analysis. The ECtHR's reasoning also caused criticism and has resulted in scholarly articles already.[312] It is always possible to discuss the reasons for why a particular judgment is reached in an individual case. The fact is that at the moment, and whilst religious pluralism—both at an individual and a group level—is hailed as something to be cherished and promoted, the ECtHR locates the interpretation of what this concretely entails and how to reconcile it with the demand that states be neutral, to a large degree—while not exclusively—with states. This is so even if cases like *Lautsi* and *S.A.S.* are, in the first place, "European-level litigation to challenge national arrangements and rules related to religion and its role in society", something which makes the ECtHR the venue for "disputes around legal and social structures that reflect particular religious traditions or particular conceptions of the limits on religion's social and legal influence".[313] As Fokas puts it, the ECtHR "has become a quasi-constitutional court for approximately 820 million individuals residing in the 47 Member States of the Council of Europe".[314]

311 *S.A.S.* v. *France*, App no 43835/11, 1 July 2014, para 122.

312 On the concept "living together", see e.g. Eva Brems, 'S.A.S. v France as a Problematic Precedent', 9 July 2014, <https://strasbourgobservers.com/2014/07/09/s-a-s-v-france-as-a-problematic-precedent/> accessed 13 June 2017; Fokas 2015, 64; Ilias Trispiotis, 'Two Interpretations of "Living Together" in European Human Rights Law' (2016) 75 *Cambridge Law Journal* 580. See further also the recent cases of *Belcacemi and Oussar* v. *Belgium*, App no 37798/13, 11 July 2017, and *Dakir* v. *Belgium*, App no 4619/12, 11 July 2017.

313 McCrea 2016, 184.

314 Fokas 2015, 55; referring to Koenig 2012.

Yet, returning to the point of legitimacy that Henrard raised with regard to the margin of appreciation, religion is of course a highly "divisive issue". Hence, it is not surprising that an international judicial body that has few if any enforcement mechanisms at its disposal and is dependent on contracting states voluntarily complying with its judgments, wishes to tread carefully and closely aligns itself with the authoritative position of states, appealing either to the consensus on a particular issue among contracting states or, where this is lacking, affords states a wide margin of appreciation, as has been the case in matters of religion to a larger extent than in many other matters.[315] Only so can the ECtHR uphold some political legitimacy and judicial authority vis-à-vis the contracting states in the matter.[316]

Finally, judge Dean Spielmann, also formerly the president of the Strasbourg court, argued a while back that the margin of appreciation is about the contracting states and the ECtHR sharing the responsibility for making human rights real.[317]

> Rather than Strasbourg deferring to the national authorities, or stopping short in its review, it devolves to the domestic level a measure of responsibility for ensuring observance of human rights. The margin of appreciation is neither a gift not a confession, therefore, but an incentive to national courts to conduct the requisite Convention review, to balance competing rights, to weigh up rights against other aspects of the public interest, and to scrutinize the proportionality of interferences with human rights. It follows that the European Court's task in such circumstances is to supervise the review conducted by the domestic courts—a European review going hand in hand with the domestic review.[318]

This may sound ideal. A risk is of course that this deference to national authorities results in an affirmation of the status quo and what Saba Mahmood has

---

315 Fokas 2015, 58; Carolyn Evans, *Freedom of Religion under the European Convention on Human Rights* (Oxford University Press 2001) 143.

316 See e.g. Pamela Slotte and Martin Scheinin, 'Captain, Fire Brigade or Icebreaker? Political Legitimacy as a Rationale in Human Rights Adjudication' in Tage Kurtén and Lars Herzberg (eds), *Legitimacy: The Treasure of Politics* (Peter Lang 2011) 89–128; Fokas 2015, 66–67; Henrard 2015, 414. "Judicial authority ultimately depends on the confidence of its citizens. If a court's interpretations deeply differ from the convictions of the people, the people will start resisting judicial decisions." Manchini 2010, 26; quoted in Fokas 2015, 67.

317 Spielmann 2014, 64.

318 Spielmann 2014, 63–64.

called "the majoritarian tilt of religious freedom law".[319] It means that majority perceptions of religion are allowed to set the crucial parameters for how faith and freedom in matters of faith is conceptualised. This is not the place for a more detailed discussion of this particular issue. The focus has been another, with the doctrine of margin of appreciation taken as a concrete example. There are naturally also other tools, for instance the legal precedents the ECtHR chooses to rely on in a specific case, which contribute to framing matters in particular ways and circumscribe or open new avenues for the exercise of judicial power on part of the ECtHR.

Increased Judicial Power over "Religious Law"

The ECtHR has also dealt with cases which in part have concerned explicit "religious law". Again, the ECtHR has made ample use of the margin of appreciation and in so doing vested power in national policy and law makers and adjudicators. However, the cases also show that in situations where national law recognizes "religious law" in a particular country, for example, following international agreements between the state and a particular church, the ECtHR assumes jurisdiction and considers the religious law in question as part of the valid law it will consider when deciding the case. The cases of *Fernández Martínez* v. *Spain*, and *Sindicatul "Păstorul cel Bun"* v. *Romania* offer examples of this, as does, for example, the more recent case of *Travaš* v. *Croatia*.[320] The ECtHR at times also make direct reference to "religious law", as it did in the last mentioned case when it made direct reference to relevant parts of the Code of Canon Law in its judgment.[321]

Similar case studies as the one which in all brevity has been carried out here with regard to the ECtHR can be found also with regard to other jurisdictions around the globe. For example, in their article on 'Regulation of "Religion" and the "Religious": The Politics of Judicialization and Bureaucratization in India and Indonesia', Sezgin and Künkler offer two additional examples of how constitutional juridification of religion has increased judicial power in the area of "religion law" and "religious law" alternatively fuelled bureaucratization of religion.[322]

---

319 Mahmood 2016, 178.

320 *Fernández Martínez* v. *Spain*, App. No. 56030/07, 15 May 2012; *Fernández Martínez* v. *Spain* [GC], App no 56030/07, 12 June 2014; *Sindicatul "Păstorul cel Bun"* v. *Romania*, App. No. 2330/09, 31 January 2012; *Sindicatul "Păstorul cel Bun"* v. *Romania* [GC]; *Travaš* v. *Croatia*, App. No. 75581/13, 4 October 2016.

321 *Travaš* v. *Croatia*, paras. 45, 91–92, 94–95.

322 Sezgin and Künkler 2014.

Issues for Further Research

Returning to the bigger picture, Ran Hirsch has in several contributions examined what he calls judicialization of politics and which takes place through the kind of "rights-jurisprudence" examined here. Deference to courts and their empowerment can take different expressions, be done for a variety of reasons—including for the purpose of shifting responsibility for contentious issues—and come about through different forms of agency, including "[l]egal mobilization from below".[323] The last issue presents us with a link between constitutive juridification A, juridification D and what Blichner and Molander titles juridification E or "legal framing", and to which we will turn next.

Before that, however, it is worth pointing out that scholars of law and religion would do well to move the gaze beyond a focus on the fuzziness of the concept of religion and how courts "close down meaning", to exploring matters of indeterminacy and lack of transparency more broadly as it pertains to litigation in religious matters. How do adjudicative bodies within different jurisdictions make use of the power vested in them? How do they navigate the thorny issues which religion cases raise and narrow in on what forms "solid ground" for decision-making, issues with regard to which they consider that they can legitimately voice themselves? How do they establish and negotiate the limits of their competence in relation to other authorities, for example "religious" ones, and how does the actual use of judicial power affect mobilisation for new or changed legislation (A/B) as well as patterns of judicial (C1) and legal solving (C2), and vice versa. The broader societal and political landscape should form an important aspect for any inquiry of the matters at hand. Moreover, law and religion scholars could fruitfully draw on other work investigating the nature of law within the fields of legal theory, legal philosophy and critical legal studies, for instance.

3E *Legal Framing*

The fifth dimension of juridification is the most difficult part of the model suggested by Blichner and Molander to substantiate empirically. Envisioned as an aggregate of the other four dimensions (A, B, C and D) juridification E occurs as a process of increased "legal framing", whereby individuals, organizations and state entities increasingly come to understand themselves and their relations

323 Hirsch 2006, 725–26. See also more generally Hirsch 2004; Hirsch 2006. An example of strategic judicialisation that Hirsch mentions is "the transfer of fundamental collective-identity or "religion and state" quandaries from the political sphere to the constitutional courts" in countries where theocratic ideas enjoy popular support yet are not backed by the political elites. Hirsch 2006, 746.

to others "in light of a common legal order".[324] Hence, individuals increasingly perceive themselves as both the addressees of law (E1) and the authors of law (E2). Drawing on Georg Jellinek's theory of status to expand on what this means in terms of legal subjectivity, Blichner and Molander distinguish between "the passive, the negative, the positive and the active status of a legal person."[325] In effect, law stands forth as the primary way to identify and safeguard individual and societal goods, such as personal freedom and social well-being and accordingly identify rights-holders (broadly speaking) and duty-bearers, effectively replacing other ways of envisioning agency and relations, for instance, in terms of moral obligations like a duty to charity.[326] Simultaneously, Blichner makes the stronger normative point in his later single-authored article that "juridification E may proceed at the expense of, or subsuming, other conceptions of the self and others, conceptions which the status of a legal person presupposes and is meant to protect." This would be juridification E carried too far, effectively undermining itself.[327]

While the passive, negative and positive status of legal personality imply the conception of individuals as addressees of law, the "active" status of legal person relates to people as authors of the law (E2). What Blichner and Molander have in mind here is the fact that "democratic participation increasingly is thought of in legal terms".[328] The end result is that legal culture comes to extend beyond the scope of other "background cultures". Law stands forth as a crucial part of sense-making, and a culture of law and legality becomes an apparatus that people cannot think without. Under these conditions, people do not turn to law strategically only for particular purposes, like simply in order to solve conflicts (juridification C); rather, law is internalised in a more comprehensive way. This means that even if persons may question the legitimacy of particular pieces of legislation or their interpretation, this will not lead them to question the legitimacy of legal culture as a whole, the principle of the rule of law nor their own generally designated status within the legal system.

---

324 Blichner and Molander 2008, 47.

325 Blichner and Molander 2008, 47; Georg Jellinek, *System der subjektiven öffentlichen Rechte* (2 Aufl., Mohr 1905).

326 Naturally there are also other ways of envisioning individuals as legal subjects, a famous way of deconstructing juridical relationships being the one of Wesley N. Hohfeld who characterises such relations in terms of immunities, liberties, rights (claim-rights), power and correlative legal obligations of various kinds. Wesley N. Hohfeld, 'Some Fundamental Legal Conceptions as Applied in Legal Reasoning' (1913) 23 *Yale Law Journal* 16.

327 He makes similar remarks with regard to the other dimensions of juridification. Blichner 2011, 30.

328 Blichner and Molander 2008, 47.

Susan S. Silbey and Ayn Cavicchi offer an example of the effects of a public sphere saturated by law where people view themselves as the addressees and authors of law when they explain how law permeates and operates in everyday life, surfacing much like an iceberg at certain points when it becomes an object of reflection, contestation and resistance.

> When we speak of the "rule of law," it is because most of the iceberg of legality lies submerged within the taken-for-granted expectations of mundane life. Rather than contested and choreographed in sometimes spectacular but always statistically rare trials, law is powerful and "rules" everyday life, because its constructions are regularly uncontested and habitual. Law's constructions and mediations have been sedimented throughout the routines of daily living, helping to make things move around in more or less clear ways, without having to invoke, display or wield their elaborate and intricate processes, especially the ultimate one, physical force. Of course, this sedimentation and normative regulation is never complete; we do not always stay within the boundaries of legally sanctioned expectations, and the reach of law is always disputed.[329]

People act upon an "everyday legal consciousness",[330] and will also verify and reinforce other dimensions of juridification in turn, as juridification E prepares the ground for conflict solving by recourse to law (juridification C) as the favored option.[331] However, such conflict solving can take many different forms, as "visible legal battles" in the formal legal system (C1) are "the outliers of the law's more routine activities." Conflict solving with more indirect (C2) or peripheral (C3) connections to the formal legal system, however, are at the heart and center of these routine activities.[332] Hence, law is crucial for sense-making not only at an individual plane, but individuals also become part of society by accepting law as the basic frame of reference, as "[t]he status as citizen is more than a formal matter."[333]

---

329 Susan S. Silbey and Ayn Cavicchi, 'The Common Place of Law: Transforming Matters of Concern into the Objects of Everyday Life' in Bruno Latour and Peter Weibel (eds), *Making Things Public: Atmospheres of Democracy* (MIT Press 2005) 556. <http://web.mit.edu/ssilbey/www/pdf/making_things_public.pdf> accessed 26 June 2017.

330 Patricia Ewick and Susan S. Silbey, *The Common Place of Law: Stories from Everyday Life* (University of Chicago Press 1998); Comaroff 2009, 195.

331 Blichner 2011, 37.

332 Silbey and Cavicchi 2005, 556.

333 Blichner and Molander 2008, 47–48.

Conversely, it also seems the case that law is ultimately dependent on processes of legal framing. As Blichner points out in his single-authored article where he elaborates ideas by Neil McCormick: "Law is democratic in the minimal sense that, if a legal order is not generally accepted by the norm-users, it cannot properly be called law (but has to be called something else, such as, for example, a coercive order). Law is limited, in the sense that, if norm-users do not freely accept and internalise a particular legal order, law will not prevail."[334] This observation does not limit this particular aspect of legal framing to only constitutional democracies. The notion of "democratic" does not per se seem to rule out religiously founded law either. The characteristics mentioned could be hallmarks of both "secular" and "religious" law.

While not coined in the same language, other scholars have made similar points as Blichner and Molander make here. In addition to those already quoted above, John Comaroff has talked of a "culture of legality", to highlight how everyday life becomes organised with reference to law. The culture of legality is a "very general phenomenon: the rising salience of the law—at once as ideology, as species of practice, as utopic cure-all, as landscape of political struggle, as instrument of governmentality—with changes in the global order of things that are often loosely glossed under the label neo-liberalism'."[335] The indicators of this culture of legality overlap with the processes of juridification as listed by Blichner and Molander: "the tidal wave of national constitutions (re)written since 1989, with their stress on the rule of law and on political, economic, social, even cultural rights"; "the emergence of new, expansive forms of 'transnational legality'; the fast development of new legal regimes; "the judicialization of politics" and "the resort to litigation to deal with an ever broader spectrum of everyday matters", and so forth.[336]

Transposed to the phenomenon of religion, what could be said about how religious life is orchestrated through law in an often unremarkable yet at points even highly contested fashion? As media coverage and public and political debate on religion is increasing worldwide, law provides a universalist vocabulary and taxonomy for the framing of issues of global concern: this legal framing can be observed in the interpretation of the advances of ISIS in Syria

---

334 Blichner 2011, 34.

335 Comaroff 2009, 193–94; Giuseppe Dalla Torre, 'A Strong Moral Conscience for a Culture of Legality', *Jubilaeum A.D. 2000*, "Tertium Millennium," No. 1, February. <http://www.vatican.va/jubilee_2000/magazine/documents/ju_mag_01021998_p-8_en.html> accessed 23 June 2017.

336 Comaroff 2009, 194–95.

and Iraq as a question of the freedom of religion or belief,[337] and the categorization of the marginalized socio-political position of minorities in the Middle East as issues of religious persecution.[338] It is even possible to see law as a "secular" medium for religion, as Comaroff points out with regard to present-day Christianity which, according to Comaroff, is "interpellating itself into the law—and, in doing so, into governance—in an effort to extend the reach of faith-based sovereignty" and here has ample historical precedence to draw on.[339]

These loose examples notwithstanding, the issue of "legal framing" remains elusive: Do the aforementioned processes of juridification A, B, C and D and their internal relationships really lead to the suppression of how other "background cultures" approach and frame religion? Can this be empirically tested? If these processes, in all their internal complexities and contradictions lead to legal framing, in which ways do they affect it? Or otherwise put, how do the process(es) of legal framing draw on the other juridification processes for their "construction", for lack of better word? In what ways do legal artefacts, practices and institutions produced and reproduced in the other dimensions of juridification, and through their interactions, contribute to the self-portrayal and agency of religious beings, individuals as well as collectives?

Given the levels of abstraction, uncertainties and simplifications inherent to the model developed by Blichner and Molander, we suggest that the applicability of legal framing as a tool with which to approach the interaction between law and religion is first and foremost theoretical in nature, providing scholars with an expanded set of terms and categories. Much like the dominant research themes within scholarship on law and religion (see part 2), the process of legal framing is inherently complicated to substantiate empirically: as an aggregate concept that is considered to be at the endpoint of a highly volatile and abstracted model of interaction, its utility for researchers is primarily at the conceptual level. With the proviso that questions of legal framing remain at the conceptual level, however, these questions would seem vital for scholars of law and religion to engage with, as they provide tools that can be "good to think with",[340] in the sense of offering useful tools with which to provide more detailed examinations of social interactions.

---

337 Hurd 2015.

338 Saba Mahmood, 'Religious Freedom, the Minority Question, and Geopolitics in the Middle East' (2012) 54 *Comparative Studies in Society and History* 418.

339 Comaroff 2009, 201.

340 The term "good to think with" is frequently attributed to Claude Lévi-Strauss, explaining the utility of concrete, tangible terms for the conceptual identification of abstract ideas. See Jonathan Culler, 'Lévi-Strauss: Good to Think With' (2013) 123 *Yale French Studies* 6.

Acting as the potential endpoint and resulting effect of preceding processes of juridification, legal framing can also be viewed as the starting points of new cycles across all the other dimensions, inspiring the adoption of new legislation and litigation in unequal measures, relative to the case at hand. Importantly, this double effect as endpoint and starting point is not limited to juridification, but may also be instrumental to processes of dejuridification: If the growth of legal regulations and ensuing increases in litigation on religion is effectively dedicated to the limitation of legal regulations of religion (see 3C), then the resulting "legal framing" of religion may be one that is more concerned with the ways in which religion should be deregulated and set free from the encumbrances of regulation and litigation.

Despite the uncertainties inherent to a concept as fuzzy as "legal framing", we suggest that scholars working at the intersections of law and religion could benefit from a deeper engagement with the interface between legal regulation and adjudication on the one hand, and dominant discourses, terms and concepts in the wider social context that law is always part of, on the other hand. While this interaction has been stressed both in the critical approach that sees law as an inevitable distortion of "lived religion" and in the theoretical developments towards a "sociology of law and religion" (see part 2), the influence of social contexts tend to be downplayed or outright ignored by most scholars working with law and religion. This criticism is in no small part directed at ourselves, as we have done the majority of our research relying mostly on more narrowly construed legal and theoretical materials, frequently at the expense of a more broadly oriented examination of how legal regulations and their adjudication generate, and in turn become affected by, its larger societal framework.

Conclusion

This article started with Walter B. Gallie's observation that religion is an "essentially contested concept", because there is no one singular definition of the term readily available. At this point it would seem pertinent to add to this fairly blunt assertion the more constructively oriented observation by Jonathan Z. Smith that the essential contestation of a concept like religion only serves as proof of the bountiful definitions that can be generated to capture one or more aspects of the concept.[341] Indeed, one would be hard pressed to find any

341 Jonathan Z. Smith, 'Religion, Religions, Religious' in Mark C. Taylor (ed), *Critical Terms for Religious Studies* (Chicago University Press 1998) 269–84, 281.

important, socially constituted concept that has a singular definition, from the inherently contested notions of culture and nation, to more prosaic elements like music or the arts.

Our aim with this article has been to recognize the scope of the challenge identified by Gallie, but also to point scholars in the direction indicated by Smith: the recognition that religion is difficult, or even impossible to define should not be viewed as an obstacle or a problem to be solved, but as an invitation to examine the broad diversity of ways in which people, systems, theories and institutions approach and conceptualize religion; to explore why they choose *this* approach to religion, rather than *that*, and how these choices draw on and inspire parallel developments in other discourses, in other places and at other times. While such explorations may be conducted in a variety of different ways, we suggest that the model of juridification developed by Blichner and Molander provides one set of available tools for scholars working at the intersections between law and religion.

Building on this, we have also tentatively identified underexplored yet timely areas of research. With regard to these, it is possible to draw on the prevalent and combined expertise of scholars working in the intersections of law and religion from empirical, comparative, historical and in various ways critical perspectives. Yet, importantly, we suggest that it will additionally encourage broadening even further the set of academic conversation partners for scholars working in the field of law and religion. As such, ours is a call for the "normalization" of scholarship on law and religion: Rather than assuming or positing the "special" or "unique" nature of this relationship, we hope that this article can help scholars identify the "everyday", "lived" and mundane interactions that happen at the intersections of law and religion.

www.ingramcontent.com/pod-product-compliance
Lightning Source LLC
Chambersburg PA
CBHW031331230926
51848CB00001B/186
9789004349629